THE POLITICS
OF ECSTASY

BY TIMOTHY LEARY, PHD.

RONIN PUBLISHING

PO BOX 22900   OAKLAND, CA 94609

www.roninpub.com

The Politics of Ecstasy

ISBN: 1-57951-031-0
ISBN: 978-1-57951-031-2
Copyright: 1980, 1985, 1993, 1998 Timothy Leary, Ph.D.

Published by
RONIN PUBLISHINNG, INC
PO Box 22900
Oakland CA 94609
www.roninpub.com

Beverly Potter—Project Editor
Judy July/Generic Type—Cover Design

Printed in the United States of America
Library of Congress Number: 2011930323

Collector's Note: The original edition of *Politics of Ecstasy* has
been divided into two books. This abbreviated edition carries
the original title of *Politics of Ecstasy* and contains Chapters
1 to 11 of the original. The remaining material appears in a
companion book entitled *Tune In Turn On Drop Out*, which
contains Chapters 12 to 22 of the original text.

Dedicated
to Abbie Hoffman

Please allow me to reintroduce this book called, so prophetically, *The Politics of Ecstasy.* I can modestly praise the magnificent, audacious, oxy-moronic, oxy-generic title because it was given to me by Abbie Hoffman, to whom I re-dedicate the book.

ECSTASY: The experience of attaining freedom from limitations, either self-imposed or external; a state of exalted delight in which normal understanding is felt to be surpassed. From the Greek "ex-stasis." By definition, ecstasy is an ongoing on/off process. It requires a continual sequence of "dropping out." On those occasions when many individuals share the ecstatic experience at the same time, they create a brief-lived "counter-culture."

SYNONYMS: Euphoria, high, rush, delight, bliss, elation, enchantment, joy, nirvana, rapture.

STASIS: Standing, a standstill

Allen Ginsberg and Timothy Leary

Steve Gladstone

Table of Contents

Foreword by Tom Robbins

If, on the face of it, the phrase, "politics of ecstasy," seems an oxymoron on the order of "wildlife management," please remember that in the Sixties virtually all political activism was connected, directly or indirectly, to the ingestion of psychedelic drugs and therefore was shaped by, if not centered in, ecstatic states of being.

In addition, there were the politics that plagued our ecstatic enterprises themselves, no matter how we twisted and squirmed to escape it. Many a commune, demonstration, or love-in wrecked on the twin shoals of property and control. Then, too, there were the political fires kindled by the friction of latter-day ecstasy cults rubbing up against the stiff hide of the old iguana-brained Establishment.

It is an understatement to write that Timothy Leary was privy to this stormy marriage of the mundane and the rapturous. Simultaneously observer and participant, Dr. Leary analyzed events around him even as he helped make them happen. Boundlessly energetic, keenly insightful, he was uniquely qualified to work both sides of Heisenberg Street. Imagine him studiously taking notes even as he skated on one foot along the vibrating rim of an indole ring.

For those whose image of Dr. Leary has been formed by shallow and often malicious reports in the press, *The Politics of Ecstasy* provides a more accurate picture of the brave neuronaut whom I believe to be the Galileo of our age, albeit a Galileo possessed of considerable Irish blarney (which makes him all the more agreeable). Of more importance, perhaps, is the light this book casts upon the century's outlaw decade at a time when Sixties revisionism is epidemic.

Whether out of ignorance of cowardice, far too many historians writing about the period are avoiding any discussion of those mind-altering substances without which the Sixties, as we know them, would never had occurred. Dr. Leary, as might be expected, leaves no turn unstoned.

Ultimately, the Sixties may be viewed as a staging area for the next leap forward in human evolution. We have left them behind only as panicky climbers might flee their base camp for a temporary descent back into the dark and decadent valley of their origins. While millions may have retreated into materialism and fundamentalism, however, Timothy Leary has continued up the mountain, his ropes coiled like a helix, his gaze on hyperspace.

For those of us who lag behind, his as-it-happened observations of where we've been are as crucial as they are entertaining. And they are entertaining, indeed, indeed.

—Tom Robbins

Introduction by R. U. Sirius

*H*ere we have *The Politics of Ecstasy*—a book that's so mid-Sixties you can virtually *smell* the incense and peppermints.

Were you there? Do you remember how tenderly and timidly even the most staid, square twentysomething of that time would loosen his tie or kick up her heels and...*swing*? Burning draft cards. Joining the Peace Corps and going native for a year or two. Wife swapping. Interracial Marriages. Mini-skirts. Smoking Pot. The Great Society. What wild chaos!

How quaint and charming it all looks to us now. Note in this book Dr. Leary's delightfully straightforward utopian idealism as he's swept up in the enthusiasm of the youthquake while still communicating about "the ancient 2-billion year old wisdom of our cells" to the *Playboy*-reading bourgeoisie. And here he is speaking with exquisite eloquence and painful earnestness about the depths of the religious quest and the need to turn one's back on the one-dimensional chessboard reality of Sixties society. "There will be green grass growing on Wall Street in ten years."

Well, no. But the Wall Street of *thirty* years hence offers visions even stranger, like Net-wired consultants manipulating fractally-constructed investment programs written by acidheads in 3-dimensional virtual reality systems to exploit a "free market" world wild and surreal beyond our best 300 microgram visions. It's not as kind and gentle—alas!—as the image of green grass growing on Wall Street. And therein lies as good a reason as any to cast back in time to this beguiling, sociopolitically naive (but admirably sophisticated in its erudite discourse on the various levels of god-intoxicated experience) collection and maybe book a round-trip ticket on trans-temporal airlines to smuggle back some of that sweet visionary stuff into the unholy chaos of now and make it just a little bit holier.

The power, voice, and vision that made Timothy Leary an American icon are embodied in *The Politics of Ecstasy* perhaps more than any other work. This book presents the "Turn On, Tune In, Drop Out" Timothy Leary of myth and legend, from the years when his influence was at its peak. When *that* Timothy Leary advised us to "drop out of the fake prop TV game" of society, he didn't anticipate the irresistible seduction of 101 channels, some of them filled with post-psychedelic hipster cynicism amplified by 124-frames-per-second flashing imagery all in the service of selling jeans and sneakers. How could *that* Timothy Leary have known about the adrenal thrills of hyper-pornographic bodies, movie-star quality cocaine, decadent trisexual glam rock star orgies, ultraviolet cinematic eyeball kicks, Donkey Kong, punk, cyberpunk, Total Distortion, gangsta, Internet, robots on Mars, virtual reality, billion dollar Silicon Valley babies, speed and chaos and chaos and *speed*— and all of it *within* the "fake-prop TV set studio" of our entirely decentered and hypermediated hallucinatory so-called "society." Do we really want to drop out on this deliriously sexy headrush?

Read *The Politics of Ecstasy*. It may indeed make you want to turn your back on it all. To TURN ON to the much grander and more elegant 2-billion year old cosmic comedy show, TUNE IN to the rhythms and harmonies within your body and the universe and the natural seasons, log off from the super-accelerated TV-prop headrush—and DROP OUT!

R. U. Sirius

Mill Valley, California

August 1998

Introduction by Timothy Leary

*T*he Sixties revolution created—and continues to create—a new, post-political society based on Ecstasy, i.e. the experience of Individual Freedom. This movement is the "rapture" anticipated for the Twenty-First Century. It is the culmination of the mystical, transcendental spooky, hallucinatory dreams which we have envisioned in our highest psychedelic (mind-opened) states.

What do we call this new movement? Humanism? Libertarianism? The Golden Age of the Individual Gods? Well, who cares what we call it. Let's loosen up. Can't we get a bit semantically loose at this moment of realization?

Oh yes, I remember. The message of the movement is FREEDOM! The medium of this movement is electronic information. Marshall McLuhan wouldn't have been surprised.

This anthem was broadcast electronically when Martin Luther King "dreamed" out loud, chanting: "Free at last. Free at last. Thank God Almighty (*sic*), free at last." Look at the faces of those assembled in that political orgy in Washington D.C., August 28, 1963. They are in ecstasy. Transported.

This chant was repeated at the First Human Be-In in San Francisco in 1967. It was sung in Paris in 1968, at Woodstock in 1969, London in 1970, Amsterdam in1971, Madrid-Barcelona in 1976. Bob Dylan sang it: We ain't gonna work on Breznev's Farm no more. They sang it at anti-war demonstrations. Hell no! We won't go! Abbie Hoffman called it *Revolution for the Hell of It*. Abbie claimed to be a Marxist—a follower of Groucho, not Karl. Rebellion with a smile.

The goals of this new Ecstatic neo-society are to support, nurture, teach, protect individual freedom and person growth. There is one and only function of neo-government in the Post-Political Age. To protect individual freedom from threats by individuals or groups who attempt to limit personal freedom.

This movement has been made possible by cybernetic-electronic technology. Mind-expanding drugs and mind-linking quantum appliances.

This individual-freedom movement is new to human history because it is not based on geography, politics, class, or religion. It has to do not with changes in the political structure, nor with who controls the police, but with the individual mind. It involves "thinking for yourself." It concerns intelligence, personal access to information, an anti-ideological reliance on common sense, mental proficiency, consciousness raising, street-smarts, good-natured sexual sophistication, intelligent consumerism, personal communication skills.

The rapid spread of this ecstatic spirit is due to the recent availability of brain-change neurotransmitters and electronic communication appliances accessible to individuals. When these psychedelic foods activate the brain and when these electronic devices start gushing electronic information, people's minds begin opening.

The signs are always the same. Young minds exposed to neurological freedom and the free spray of electronic information suddenly blossom like flowers in the spring.

The first psychedelic-cybernetic generation in human history, individuals who prize intelligence and facts and personal freedom. These are young people who grew up with electronic appliances, personal telephones, home radios, television and personal computers as primary aids for thinking and communicating. From birth they have been trained by television to be reality-consumers. To have freedom of choice.

Power, Mao said, comes from the barrel of a gun. That may have been true in the past. At the cusp of the Twenty-First Century, the notion of political "power" seems anachronistic, kinky, hateful, evil. The idea that any group should want to grab domination, control, authority, supremacy, jurisdiction over others is a primitive perversity—more loathsome than cannibalism. A return to personal or economic slavery. The issue now is personal power, i.e. freedom. And now we see that freedom depends upon who controls the technology that reaches your brain-telephone, the editing facility, the drugs, of course, and the TV screen.

This sudden emergence of Pro-Choice on a mass scale is new. In TRIBAL societies the role of the individual is to be a submissive, obedient child. The tribal elders do the thinking. And survival pressures do not afford them the luxury of freedom.

In FEUDAL societies the individual is a serf or vassal, peasant, chattel, peon, slave. The nobles and priests do the thinking. And they are trained by tradition to abhor and anathematize open-mindedness and thinking for yourself.

In an INDUSTRIAL society the individual is a worker-manager. In later stages, the individual is worker-consumer. In all of these static, primitive societies the thinking is done by organizations who control the guns. The power of Open-Minded Individuals to make and remake their own lives is severely limited.

The INFORMATION society, which we are now developing, is post-political, and does not operate on the basis of obedience and conformity to dogma. It is based upon individual thinking, scientific know-how, quick exchange of facts, high-tech ingenuity, and practical, front-line creativity.

The society of the future will no longer grudgingly tolerate a few open-minded innovators. The Info-Society is totally dependent upon a large pool of them, communicating with each other across state lines and national boundaries.

When we send electrified thoughts this way, inviting fast feedback, we are creating a new global psyber-society which requires a higher level of electronic know-how and psychological sophistication. This psyber-communication process is accelerating so rapidly that to compete on the world information market in the Twenty-First Century, nations, companies, even families (!) must be composed of quick-thinking, open-minded, change-oriented, innovative individuals who are adept in communicating via the new cyber-electronic technologies.

These free men and free women are simply much smarter than the Old Guard. They inhale new information the way they breathe oxygen. They stimulate each other to continually upgrade and reformat their

[7

minds. People who use psyber-technology to make fast decisions on their jobs are not going to go home and passively let aging, close-minded politicians or devil-obsessed, religious demagogues make decisions about their lives.

The emergence of this new open-minded caste in different countries around the world is the central historical issue of the last forty years. Back in 1967, we called this process of personal freedom the Ecstatic Experience. Today we call the free-agent who thinks for him/herself "cybernetic" from the Greek word for pilot. The word "psychedelic" means ecstatic or mind-opening. "Psybernetic" refers to psychedelic experience expressed in electronic form. The Japanese word "ronin" is also used to describe the highly skilled, self-confident free-agent who has renounced vassal, liege service to a Lord and launched out on an individual path within a rigidly structured world.

In the 1950s in America there appeared such a group of free people who created a counter-culture which was to change history. They were called "The Beat Generation." Their spokesperson was the poet Allen Ginsberg. Their philosopher hero was William Burroughs. They were anarchist artists and writers. They hung out with avant garde painters and jazz musicians. They stood, of course, for the ecstatic vision and for individual freedom in revolt against all bureaucratic, close-minded systems. They saw themselves as citizens of the world. They met with Russian poets to denounce the Cold War. They practiced oriental yoga. They experimented, as artists have for centuries, with mind-opening foods, drugs, sexual freedom. Most important, with their minds turning like satellite dishes to other cultures, they had a historical sense of what they were doing. They saw themselves as heirs to the long tradition of intellectual and artistic individualism that goes beyond national boundaries.

What made the Beats more effective than any dissident artist group in human history was electronic technology. Their ideas and their images were broadcast at the speed of light around the world. Just as soap companies were using TV and radio to market their products, so did the Beats used the electronic media to advertise their ideas. Ironically enough, more students in China and the Third World know the name Allen Ginsberg today than any other American writer. Allen was the king of the Czechoslovakian Students May Day parade in Prague, of all places, in 1964. The next day, after the party officials realized what Allen had in mind for Czech youth, they promptly deported him.

Talk about the Politics of Ecstasy! The original Love-In-Be-In (San Francisco, January 1967) was the dawning of the Psychedelic-Cybernetic Age.

This first Love-In-Be-In was not organized in the traditional way. The word got out via the underground presses and progressive, free-form radio stations. When Jerry Rubin jumped on stage and tried to run a political scam, no one listened. Three months later the Pop Festival in Montery, California harnessed the new youthful psychedelic spirit to electronically amplified music.

Ecstatic Youth plus electronics.

The first edition of *The Politics of Ecstasy* appeared in 1968. The first wave of post-Hiroshima electronic children had recently reached the age of twenty-one. *The Politics of Ecstasy* was a dramatic departure from the previous texts we sober Harvard psychometricians had written about the consciousness-expanding foods and drugs. *The Psychedelic Experience* and *Psychedelic Reader* were scholarly texts based on ancient shamanic tradition and designed to guide mature, thoughtful seekers.

The Politics of Ecstasy was written for the enormous new wave of young people, the first generation of the television age, who were used to "turning-on-tuning-in" electronic appliances. It was written to provide a supportive "set" for the millions of psychedelic users who were learning how to live free. Much of it was written in a state of rapturous delusion.

I used the term "politics" to focus on the cultural-social implications of the psychedelic experience. This was considered by the conventional wisdom to be naive. Politics of ecstasy?

By 1969 the power of the youth movement and the counter-culture press and underground radio drew 500,000 to Woodstock, New York and later to the Anti-War demonstrations.

I did actually try to put the post-politics of ecstasy into practice. I announced my candidacy for governor of California in 1969. My opponent was Ronald Reagan who was amusing.

When asked what I would do if I were to become governor I replied: "As little as possible. Managing a state is like managing a baseball team. The function of the couch is to motivate, tutor, counsel, to promote team work. And, above all, to stay out of the limelight and let the performers be the stars."

Jeez! No wonder Reagan threw me in jail without bail. Once again I was ahead of my time. Promoting decentralization and regionalism some odd dangerous years before we ended the cold war.

In the societies of the past the notion of a "politics of ecstasis" was oxymoronic. How could there be a society of singular individuals who keep dropping out of the central, normal social structure?

Granted, that in most tribal societies a few persons were permitted to live out the shamanic path of exalted mysticism. And on certain festival occasions they led the tribe in ceremonies of trance, possession, and rapturous delight. Usually in devotion to the reigning god.

In Feudal and Industrial cultures the ecstatic experience was cruelly alienated from organized religions. The shamanic role was relegated to outcastes like bohemians, artists, comics, prostitutes, screenwriters, entertainers. This small, dissident, re-sourceful minority was allowed to circulate innovative, iconoclastic, creative fabrications.

The Ecstatic Beats of the 1950s, the Blissed Out Students of the 1960s, the Anarchist Yippies of the 1970s, the Cyberpunks of the 1980s, and the Ravers of the 1990s have been fabricating the Cyber Culture.

In the cybernetic Twenty-First Century power will come, not from the barrel of a gun, but from the minds of free individuals using camera lenses, computer screens, and electronic networks. Question authority and just say "Know"!

Timothy Leary
The Other Side
August 1998

Cellular level of consciousness: the message of DNA. *Terrell P. Watson*

Cellular level of consciousness: the message of DNA. *Terrell P. Watson*

1

The Seven Tongues
of God*

The Turn-On

Once upon a time, many years ago, on a sunny afternoon in the garden of a Cuernavaca villa, I ate seven of the so-called sacred mushrooms which had been given to me by a scientist from the University of Mexico. During the next five hours, I was whirled through an experience which could be described in many extravagant metaphors but which was, above all and without question, the deepest religious experience of my life.

Statements about personal reactions, however passionate, are always relative to the speaker's history and may have little general significance. Next come the questions "Why?" and "So what?"

There are many predisposing factors—intellectual, emotional, spiritual, social—which cause one person to be ready for a dramatic mind-opening experience and which lead another to shrink back from new levels of awareness. The discovery that the human brain possesses an infinity of potentialities and can operate at unexpected space-time dimensions left me feeling exhilarated, awed, and quite convinced that I had awakened

---

* Lecture delivered at a meeting of Lutheran psychologists and other interested professionals, sponsored by the Board of Theological Education, Lutheran Church in America, in conjunction with the Seventy-first Annual Convention of the American Psychological Association, Bellevue Stratford Hotel, Philadelphia, August 30, 1963; later published in *Psychedelic Review*, No. 3, 1964.

from a long ontological sleep. This sudden flash awakening is called "turning on."

Tuning In

A profound transcendent experience should leave in its wake a changed man and a changed life. Since my illumination of August 1960, I have devoted most of my energies to trying to understand the relevatory potentialities of the human nervous system and to making these insights available to others.

I have repeated this biochemical and (to me) sacramental ritual several hundred times, and almost every time I have been awed by religious revelations as shattering as the first experience. During this period I have been lucky enough to collaborate in this work with several hundred scientists and scholars who joined our various research projects. In our centers at Harvard, in Mexico, and at Millbrook we have arranged transcendent experiences for several thousand persons from all walks of life, including more than 200 full-time religious professionals, about half of whom profess the Christian or Jewish faiths and about half of whom belong to Eastern religions.

Included in this roster are several divinity college deans, divinity college presidents, university chaplains, executives of religious foundations, prominent religious editors, and several distinguished religious philosophers. In our research files and in certain denominational offices there is building up a large and quite remarkable collection of reports which will be published when the political atmosphere becomes more tolerant. At this point it is conservative to state that over 75 percent of these subjects report intense mystico-religious responses, and considerably more than 50 percent claim that they have had the deepest spiritual experience of their life.

The interest generated by the research at Harvard led to the formation in 1962 of an informal group of ministers, theologians and religious psychologists who met once a month. In addition to arranging for spiritually oriented psychedelic sessions and discussing prepared papers, this group provided the guides for the dramatic "Good Friday" study and was the original planning nucleus of the organizations which assumed sponsorship of our research in consciousness expansion: IFIF (the International Federation for Internal Freedom), 1963, the Castalia Foundation, 1963–66, and the League for Spiritual Discovery, 1966. The generating impulse and the original leadership of our work and play came from a seminar in religious experience, and this fact may be related to the alarm which we have aroused in some secular and psychiatric circles.

The Good Friday Miracle

The "Good Friday" study, which has been sensationalized recently in the press as "The Miracle of Marsh Chapel," deserves further elaboration not only as an example of a serious, controlled experiment involving over 30 courageous volunteers but also as a systematic demonstration of the religious aspects of the psychedelic revelatory experience. This study was the Ph.D. dissertation research of Walter Pahnke, at that time a graduate student in the philosophy of religion at Harvard University. Pahnke, who is, incidentally, both an M.D. and a bachelor of divinity, set out to determine whether the transcendent experience reported during psychedelic sessions was similar to the mystical experience reported by saints and famous religious mystics.

The subjects in this study were 20 divinity students selected from a group of volunteers. The subjects were divided into 5 groups of 4 persons, and each group met before the session for orientation and preparation. To each group were assigned 2 guides with considerable psychedelic experience. The 10 guides were professors and advanced graduate students from Boston-area colleges.

The experiment took place in a small, private chapel at Boston University, beginning about one hour before noon on Good Friday. The dean of the chapel, Howard Thurman, who was to conduct a 3-hour devotional service upstairs in the main hall of the church, visited the subjects a few minutes before the start of the service at noon and gave a brief inspirational talk.

Two of the subjects in each group and one of the two guides were given a moderately stiff dosage (i.e., 30 mg.) of psilocybin, the chemical synthesis of the active ingredient in the "sacred mushroom" of Mexico. The remaining two subjects and the second guide received a placebo which produced noticeable somatic side effects but which was not psychedelic. The study was triple blind: neither the subjects, guides, nor experimenter knew who received psilocybin.

A detailed description of this fascinating study can be found in Pahnke's thesis, available from the Harvard Library.[1] I can say, in summary, that the results clearly support the hypothesis that, with adequate preparation and in an environment which is supportive and religiously meaningful, subjects who have taken the psychedelic drug report mystical experiences significantly more than placebo controls.

Our studies, naturalistic and experimental, thus demonstrate that if the expectation, preparation, and setting are spiritual, an intense mystical or revelatory experience can be expected in from 40 to 90 percent of subjects ingesting psychedelic drugs. These results *may be* attributed to the bias of our research group, which has taken the "far out" and rather dangerous position that there are experiential-spiritual as well as secular-behavioral potentialities of the nervous system. While we share and follow the epistemology of scientific psychology (objective records), our basic ontological assumptions are closer to Jung than to Freud, closer to the mystics than to the theologians, closer to Einstein and Bohr than to Newton. In order to check on this bias, let us cast a comparative glance at the work of other research groups in this field who begin from more conventional ontological bases.

LSD Can Produce a Religious High

Oscar Janiger, a psychiatrist, and William McGlothlin, a psychologist, have reported the reactions of 194 psychedelic subjects. Of these, 73 took LSD as part of a psychotherapy program, and 121 were volunteers. The religious "set" would not be expected to dominate the expectations of these subjects. The results, which are abstracted from a paper published in the *Psychedelic Review*,[2] are as follows:

ITEM	PERCENT Janiger-McGlothlin (nonreligious setting) N = 194
Increased interest in morals, ethics:	35
Increased interest in other universal concepts (meaning of life) :	48
Change in sense of values	48
LSD should be used for	
becoming aware of oneself:	75
getting new meaning to life:	58
getting people to understand each other:	42
An experience of lasting benefit:	58

Two other studies, one by Ditman *et al.*, another by Savage *et al.*, used the same questionnaire, allowing for interexperiment comparison. Both Ditman and Savage are psychiatrists, but the clinical environment of the latter's study is definitely more religious (subjects are shown religious articles during the session, etc.) . Summarizing the religious items of their questionnaires:

ITEM	PERCENT	
	Ditman (supportive environment) N = 74	Savage (supportive environment & some religious stimuli) N = 96
Feel it [LSD] was the greatest thing that ever happened to me:	49	85
A religious experience:	32	83
A greater awareness of God or a higher power, or an ultimate reality:	40	90

Here, then, we have five scientific studies by qualified investigators—the four naturalistic studies by Leary *et al.*,[3] Savage *et al.*,[4] Ditman *et al.*,[5] and Janiger-McGlothlin,[6] and the triple-blind study in the Harvard dissertation mentioned earlier—yielding data which indicate that (1) if the setting is supportive but not spiritual, between 40 to 75 percent of psychedelic subjects will report intense and life-changing religious experiences and that (2) if the set and setting are supportive and spiritual, then from 40 to 90 percent of the experiences will be revelatory and mystico-religious.

It is hard to see how these results can be disregarded by those who are concerned with spiritual growth and religious development. These data are even more interesting because the experiments took place at a time (1962) when mysticism, individual religious ecstasy (as opposed to religious behavior), was highly suspect and when the classic, direct, nonverbal means of revelation and consciousness expansion such as meditation, yoga, fasting, monastic withdrawal and sacramental foods and drugs were surrounded by an aura of fear, clandestine secrecy, active social sanction, and even imprisonment.[7] The two hundred professional workers in religious vocations who partook of psychedelic substances (noted earlier) were responsible, respected, thoughtful, and moral individuals who were grimly aware of the controversial nature of the procedure and aware that their reputations and their jobs might be undermined (and, as a matter of fact, have been and are today being threatened for some of them). *Still* the results read: 75 percent spiritual revelation. It may well be that the most intense religious experience, like the finest metal, requires fire, the "heat" of police constabulatory opposition, to produce the keenest edge. When the day comes—as it surely will—that sacramental biochemicals like LSD will be as routinely and tamely used as organ music and incense to assist in the attainment of religious experience, it may well be that the ego-shattering effect of the drug will be diminished. Such may be one aspect of the paradoxical nature of religious experience.

What Is the Religious Experience?

The Religious Experience

You are undoubtedly wondering about the meaning of this phrase, which has been used so freely in the preceding paragraphs. May I offer a definition?

The religious experience is the ecstatic, incontrovertibly certain, subjective discovery of answers to seven basic spiritual questions. There can be, of course, absolute subjective certainty in regard to secular questions: Is this the girl I love? Is Fidel Castro a wicked man? Are the Yankees the best baseball team? But issues which do not involve the seven basic questions belong to secular games, and such convictions and faiths, however deeply held, can be distinguished from the religious. Liturgical practices, rituals, dogmas, theological speculations, can be and too often are secular, i.e., completely divorced from the spiritual experience.

What are these 7 basic spiritual questions?

1. *The Ultimate Power Question*

What is the basic energy underlying the universe—the ultimate power that moves the galaxies and nucleus of the atom? Where and how did it all begin? What is the cosmic plan? Cosmology.

2. *The Life Question*

What is life? Where and how did it begin? How is it evolving? Where is it going? Genesis, biology, evolution, genetics.

3. *The Human Being Question*

Who is man? Whence did he come? What is his structure and function? Anatomy and physiology.

4. *The Awareness Question*

How does man sense, experience, know? Epistemology, neurology.

5. *The Ego Question*

Who am I? What is my spiritual, psychological, social place in the plan? What should I do about it? Social psychology.

6. *The Emotional Question*

What should I feel about it? Psychiatry. Personality psychology.

7. *The Ultimate Escape Question*

How do I get out of it? Anesthesiology (amateur or professional) . Eschatology.

While one may disagree with the wording, I think most thoughtful people—philosophers or not—can agree on something like this list of basic issues. Do not most of the great religious statements—Eastern or monotheistic—speak directly to these questions?

Now one important fact about these questions is that they are continually being answered and reanswered, not only by all the religions of the world but also by the data of the natural sciences. Read these questions again from the standpoint of the goals of (1) astronomy-physics, (2) biochemistry, genetics, paleontology, and evolutionary theory, (3) anatomy and physiology, (4) neurology, (5) sociology, psychology, (6) psychiatry, (7) eschatological theology and anesthesiology.

We are all aware of the unhappy fact that both science and religion are too often diverted toward secular-game goals. Various pressures demand that laboratory and church forget these basic questions and instead provide distractions, illusory protection, narcotic comfort. Most of us dread confrontation with the answers to these basic questions, whether the answers come from objective science or religion. But if "pure" science and religion address themselves to the same basic questions, what is the distinction between the two disciplines? Science is the systematic attempt to record and measure the energy process and the sequence of energy transformations we call life. The goal is to answer the basic questions in terms of objective, observed, public data. Religion is the systematic attempt to provide answers *to the same questions* subjectively, in terms of direct, incontrovertible, personal experience.

Science is a social system which evolves roles, rules, rituals, values, language, space-time locations to further the quest for these goals, to answer these questions objectively, externally. Religion is a social system which has evolved its roles, rules, rituals, values, language, space-time locations to further the pursuit of the same goals, to answer these questions subjectively through the revelatory experience. A science which fails to address itself to these spiritual goals, which accepts other purposes (however popular), becomes secular, political, and tends to oppose new data. A religion which fails to provide direct experiential answers to these spiritual questions (which fails to produce the ecstatic high) becomes secular, political, and tends to oppose the individual revelatory confrontation. The Oxford orientalist R. C. Zaehner, whose formalism is not always matched by his tolerance, has remarked that experience, when divorced from dogma, often leads to absurd and wholly irrational excesses.[8] Like any statement of polarity, the opposite is equally true: dogma, when divorced from experience, often leads to absurd and wholly rational excesses. Those of us who have been devoting our lives to the study of consciousness have been able to collect considerable sociological data about the tendency of the rational mind to spin out its own interpretations. But I shall have more to say about the political situation in later chapters.

Religion and Science Provide Similar Answers to the Same Basic Questions

At this point I should like to advance the hypothesis that *those aspects of the psychedelic experience which subjects report to be ineffable and ecstatically religious involve a direct awareness of the energy processes which physicists and biochemists and physiologists and neurologists and psychologists and psychiatrists measure.*

We are treading here on very tricky ground. When we read the reports of LSD subjects, we are doubly limited. First, *they* can only speak in the vocabulary they know, and for the most part they do not possess the lexicon and training of energy scientists. Second, *we researchers* find only what we are prepared to look for, and too often we think in crude psychological-jargon concepts: moods, emotions, value judgments, diagnostic categories, social pejoratives, religious clichés.

Since 1962 I have talked to thousands of LSD trippers, mystics, saddhus, occultists, saints, inquiring if their hallucinations, visions, revelations, ecstasies, orgasms, hits, flashes, spaceouts, and freak-outs can be translated into the language not just of religion, psychiatry and psychology but also of the physical and biological sciences.

1. The Ultimate-Power Question

A. *The scientific answers* to this question change constantly—Newtonian laws, quantum indeterminacy, atomic structure, nuclear structure. Today the *basic energy* is located within the nucleus. Inside the atom

> a transparent sphere of emptiness, thinly populated with electrons, the substance of the atom has shrunk to a core of unbelievable smallness: enlarged 1000 million times, an atom would be about the size of a football, but its nucleus would still be hardly visible—a mere speck of dust at the center. Yet that nucleus radiates a powerful electric field which holds and controls the electrons around it.[9]

Incredible power and complexity operating at speeds and spatial dimensions which our conceptual minds cannot register. Infinitely small, yet pulsating outward through enormous networks of electrical forces—atom, molecule, cell, planet, star: all forms dancing to the nuclear tune.

The *cosmic design* is this network of energy whirling through space-time. More than 15,000 million years ago the oldest known stars began to form. Whirling disks of gas molecules (driven, of course, by that tiny, spinning, nuclear force) —condensing clouds, further condensations—the tangled web of spinning magnetic fields clustering into stellar forms, and each stellar cluster hooked up in a magnetic dance with its planetary cluster and with every other star in the galaxy, and each galaxy whirling in synchronized relationship to the other galaxies.

One thousand million galaxies. From 100 million to 100,000 million stars in a galaxy—that is to say, 100,000 million planetary systems per galaxy, and each planetary system slowly wheeling through the stellar cycle that allows for a brief time the possibility of life as we know it.

Five thousand million years ago, a slow-spinning dwarf star

we call the sun is the center of a field of swirling planetary material. The planet earth is created. In 5,000 million years the sun's supply of hydrogen will be burned up; the planets will be engulfed by a final solar explosion. Then the ashen remnants of our planetary system will spin silently through the dark infinity of space. And then is the dance over? Hardly. Our tiny solar light, which is one of 100,000 million suns in our galaxy, will scarcely be missed. And our galaxy is one of 1,000 million galaxies spinning out and up at rates which exceed the speed of light—each galaxy eventually burning up, to be replaced by new galaxies to preserve the dance equilibrium.

Here in the always changing data of nuclear physics and astronomy is the current scientific answer to the first basic question—material enough indeed for an awesome cosmology.

B. *Psychedelic reports* often contain phrases which seem to describe similar phenomena, subjectively experienced.

(a)   I passed in and out of a state several times where I was so relaxed that I felt open to a total flow, over and around and through my body (more than my body). . . . All objects were dripping, streaming, with white-hot light or electricity which flowed in the air. It was as though we were watching the world, just having come into being, cool off, its substance and form still molten and barely beginning to harden.

(b)   Body being destroyed after it became so heavy as to be unbearable. Mind wandering, ambulating throughout an ecstatically lit, indescribable landscape. How can there be so much light—layers and layers of light, light upon light? All is illumination.

(c)   I became more and more conscious of vibrations—of the vibrations in my body, the harp strings giving forth their individual tones. Gradually I felt myself becoming one with the cosmic vibration. . . . In this dimension there were no forms, no deities or personalities—just bliss.

(d)   The dominant impression was that of entering into the very marrow of existence. . . . It was as if each of the billion atoms of experience which under normal circum-

stances are summarized and averaged into crude, indiscriminate, wholesale impressions was now being seen and
savored for itself. The other clear sense was that of cosmic
relativity. Perhaps all experience never gets summarized
in any inclusive overview. Perhaps all there is, is this
everlasting congeries of an infinite number of discrete
points of view, each summarizing the whole from its perspective.

(e)   I could see the whole history and evolution along which
man has come. I was moving into the future and saw the
old cycle of peace and war, good times and bad times,
starting to repeat, and I said, "The same old thing again.
Oh, God! It has changed, though, it is different," and I
thought of the rise of man from animal to spiritual being.
But I was still moving into the future, and I saw the whole
planet destroyed and all history, evolution, and human
efforts being wiped out in this one ultimate destructive
act of God.

Subjects speak of participating in and merging with pure
(i.e., content-free) energy, white light; of witnessing the breakdown of macroscopic objects into vibratory patterns, visual nets,
the collapse of external structure into wave patterns, the awareness that everything is a dance of particles, sensing the smallness
and fragility of our system, visions of the void, of world-ending
explosions, of the cyclical nature of creation and dissolution, etc.
Now I need not apologize for the flimsy inadequacy of these
words. We just don't have a better experiential vocabulary. If
God were to permit you a brief voyage into the divine process,
let you whirl for a second into the atomic nucleus or spin you
out on a light-year trip through the galaxies, how on earth
would you describe what you saw when you got back, breathless,
to your office? This metaphor may sound farfetched or irrelevant, but just ask someone who has taken a heavy dose of LSD.

2. The Life Question

A. *The Scientific Answer:*
Our planetary system began over 5 billion years ago and has
around 5 billion years to go. Life as we know it dates back 2

billion years. In other words, the earth spun for about 60 percent of its existence without life. The crust slowly cooled and was eroded by incessant water flow. "'Fertile mineral mud was deposited . . . now giving . . . for the first time . . . the possibility of harboring life." Thunderbolts in the mud produce amino acids, the basic building blocks of life. Then begins the ceaseless production of protein molecules, incalculable in number, forever combining into new forms. The variety of proteins "exceeds all the drops of water in all the oceans of the world." Then protoplasm. Cell. Within the cell, incredible beauty and order.

> When we consider the teeming activity of a modern city it is difficult to realize that in the cells of our bodies infinitely more complicated processes are at work—ceaseless manufacture, acquisition of food, storage, communication and administration. . . . All this takes place in superb harmony, with the cooperation of all the participants of a living system, regulated down to the smallest detail.[10]

Life is the striving cycle of repetitious, reproductive energy transformations. Moving, twisting, devouring, changing. The unit of life is the cell. And the blueprint is the genetic code, the two nucleic acids—the long, intertwined, duplicating chains of DNA and the controlling regulation of RNA—"which determine the structure of the living substance."

And where is it going? Exactly like the old Hindu myths of cyclical rotation, the astrophysicists tell us that life is a temporary sequence which occurs at a brief midpoint in the planetary cycle. Terrestrial life began around 3 billion years A.B. ("after the beginning" of our solar cycle) and will run for another 2 billion years or so. At that time the solar furnace will burn so hot that the minor planets (including earth) will boil, bubble and burn out. In other planetary systems the time spans are different, but the cycle is probably the same.

There comes an intermediate stage in the temperature history of a planet which can nourish living forms, and then life merges into the final unifying fire. Data here, indeed, for an awesome cosmology.

The flame of life which moves every living form, including the cell cluster you call your *self*, began, we are told, as a tiny single-celled spark in the lower Precambrian mud, then passed over in steady transformations to more complex forms. We like to speak of higher forms, but let's not ignore or patronize the single-cell game. It's still quite thriving, thank you. Next, your ancestral fire glowed in seaweed, algae, flagellate, sponge, coral (about 1 billion years ago) ; then fish, fern, scorpion, milliped (about 600 million years ago). Every cell in your body traces back (about 450 million years ago) to the same light life flickering in amphibian (and what a fateful and questionable decision to leave the sea—should we have done it?) . Then forms, multiplying in endless diversity—reptile, insect, bird—until, 1 million years ago, comes the aureole glory of Australopithecus.*

The torch of life next passes on to the hand-ax culture (around 600,000 years ago) , to Pithecanthropus (can you remember watching for the charge of southern elephants and the saber-tooth tiger?) , then blazing brightly in the radiance of our great-grandfather Neanderthal man (a mere 70,000 years ago) , suddenly flaring up in that cerebral explosion that doubled the cortex of our grandfather Cro-Magnon man (44,000 to 10,000 years ago) , and then radiating into the full flame of recent man, our older stone age, Neolithic brothers, our bronze and iron age selves.

What next? The race, far from being culminated, has just begun:

> The development of Pre-hominines Australopithecus . . . to the first emergence of the . . . Cromagnons lasted about . . . fifteen thousand human life-spans. . . . In this relatively short period in world history the hominid type submitted to a positively hurricane change of form; indeed he may be looked upon as one of the animal groups whose potentialities of unfolding with the greatest intensity have been realized. It must,

* The fossils of the newly discovered "Homo Habilis" from East Africa are estimated to be 1,750,000 years old. (*New York Times*, March 18, April 3 and 4, 1964. Another estimate traces human origins back about 15 million years!— *New York Times*, April 12, 1964.)

however, by no means be expected that this natural flood of development will dry up with *Homo sapiens recens.* Man will be unable to remain man as we know him now, a modern sapiens type. He will in the courses of the next hundreds of millennia presumably change considerably physiologically and physically.[11]

B. *The Psychedelic Correlates* of these evolutionary and genetic concepts are to be found in the reports of almost every LSD tripper. The experience of being a one-celled creature tenaciously flailing, the singing, humming sound of life exfoliating; you are the DNA code spinning out multicellular aesthetic solutions. You directly and immediately experience invertebrate joy; you feel your backbone forming; gills form. You are a fish with glistening gills, the sound of ancient fetal tides murmuring the rhythm of life. You stretch and wriggle in mammalian muscular strength, loping, powerful, big muscles; you sense hair growing on your body as you leave the warm broth of water and take over the earth.

The psychedelic experience is the Hindu-Buddha reincarnation theory experimentally confirmed in your own nervous system. You re-experience your human forebears, shuttle down the chain of DNA remembrance. It's all there in your cellular diaries. You are all the men and women who fought and fed and met and mated—the ugly, the strong, the sly, the mean, the wise, the beautiful. Our fathers, who art protein in heaven—within; and our round-fleshed holy mothers, hallowed be thy names. Endless chain of warm-blooded, sweating, perfumed-smelling, tenaciously struggling primates, each rising out of darkness to stand for one second in the sunlight and hand on the precious electrical tissue flame of life.

What does all that evolutionary reincarnation business have to do with you or me or LSD or the religious experience? It might, it just might, have a lot to do with very current events. Many, and I am just bold enough to say most, LSD subjects say they experience early forms of racial or subhuman species evolution during their sessions. Now the easiest interpretation is the psychiatric: "Oh, yes, hallucinations. Everyone knows that LSD makes you crazy, and your delusions can take any psychotic form." But wait; not so fast. Is it entirely inconceivable that our cortical cells or the machinery inside the cellular nucleus "remember" back along the unbroken chain of electrical transformations that connects every one of us back to that original thunderbolt in the Precambrian mud? Impossible, you say? Read a genetics text. Read and reflect about the DNA chain of complex protein molecules that took you as a unicelled organism at the moment of your conception and planned every stage of your natural development. Half of that genetic blueprint was handed to you intact by your mother and half by your father, and then slammed together in that incredible welding process we call conception.

"You," your ego, your good old American social self, have been trained to remember certain crucial secular-game landmarks: your senior prom, your wedding day. But is it not possible that others of your 10 billion brain cells "remember" other critical survival crossroads, like conception, intrauterine events, birth? Events for which our language has few or no descriptive terms? Every cell in your body is the current carrier of an energy torch which traces back through millions of generation transformations. Remember that genetic code?

You must recognize by now the difficulty of my task. I am trying to expand your consciousness, break through your macroscopic, secular set, "turn you on," give you a faint feeling of a psychedelic moment, trying to relate two sets of processes for which we have no words—speed-of-light energy-transformation processes and the transcendent vision.

3. The Human Being Question

A. *The Scientific Answer*

What is the human being? Ancient riddle, usually answered from within the homocentric limits of the parochial mind. But consider this question from the perspective of an intelligence outside the "romantic fallacy" of man's superiority. Study the question from the vantage point of an outer-space visitor, or from that of an ecstatic, objective scientist.

Let us define man as man defines other species, by his anatomy and physiology. Man is an evolutionary form emerging from animal-mammalian-primate stock, characterized by this skeletal structure and these unique hematological, endocrine, organ systems.

Like every living creature, man is a seed carrier, a soul bearer made in one of the forms of God. Man's particular form is a bag of semihairless skin containing a miraculously complex system of life functions which he dimly understands in the language of physiology, functions of which he has no direct experience.

Only a rare, turned-on visionary like Buckminister Fuller can appreciate the universe of the human body, the galactic scope of somatic experience.

"Our individual brains have a quadrillion times a quadrillion atoms in fantastic coordination. . . . I think we are all coming out of the womb of very fundamental ignorance, mental ignorance. We talk in ways that sometimes sound very faithful to our experience but which are many times very imaginary. . . . We think that we know quite a lot and are responsible for a lot of what is going on.

"I say to you, whatever the last meal you ate, you haven't the slightest idea of what you are doing with it. You aren't consciously saying to yourself that 'I have designed and decided now I'm going to have a million hairs, and they're going to be such and such a shape and color.' We don't do any of this; it is all automated. Man is more than ninety-nine percent automated, and he is only a very small fraction conscious. Whereas he tends to suggest that he is really highly responsible for what goes on . . . he is very successful despite his ignorance and vanity.

"I would suggest that all of humanity is about to be born in an entirely new relationship to the universe. . . . We're going to have to have an integrity . . . a good faith with the truth, whatever the truth may be. We are going to have to really pay attention." (Buckminister Fuller, interviewed in the San Francisco *Oracle*, Vol. 1, No. 11.)

B. *The Psychedelic Correlates*

The key phrases in this typical flash of humorous genius by Buckminister Fuller are: "faithful to our experience," "automated . . . only a very small fraction conscious," "pay attention."

This is classic psychedelic talk. One of the ecstatic horrors of the LSD experience is the sudden confrontation with your own body, the shattering resurrection of your body. You are capitulated into the matrix of quadrillions of cells and somatic communication systems. Cellular flow. You are swept down the tunnels and canals of your own waterworks. Visions of microscopic processes. Strange, undulating tissue patterns. Pummeled down the fantastic artistry of internal factories, recoiling with fear or shrieking in pleasure at the incessant push, struggle, drive of the biological machinery, clicking, clicking, endlessly, endlessly—at every moment engulfing you.

Your body is the universe. The ancient wisdom of gnostics, hermetics, sufis, Tantric gurus, yogis, occult healers. What is without is within. Your body is the mirror of the macrocosm. The kingdom of heaven is within you. Within your body, body, body. The great psychedelic philosophies of the East—Tantra, Kundalini yoga—see the human body as the sacred temple, the seed center, the exquisitely architected shrine of all creation.

Hoc est corpus meum

And the systematic, disciplined awareness of body function is the basic sacramental method of these religions. Tibetan and Indian Tantra train the student to become faithful to somatic experience, to pay attention to the energies and messages of the body. Breathing, control of circulation, control of involuntary muscles and reflexes, control of digestion, control of genital erection and ejaculation, awareness of the intricate language of hormone and humor, the psychopharmacology of the body, the cakras.

One cannot understand the rhythms and meanings of the outer world until one has mastered the dialects of the body.

What is man? He is within His body. His body is his universe.

4. The Awareness Question

A. *The Scientific Answer*

Everything that man knows is mediated by the human nervous system. Everything that man knows about the external world and his place, his identity in it, comes through the sense organs.

Neurologists and sensory physiologists have much to tell us about the incredible complexity of the sensory mechanisms. The eye responding to light, the auditory system trembling to the finest variation in air vibrations, the olfactory organs receiving and processing airborne scents, the mouth and tongue honeycombed with taste buds. Touch. Temperature. Pain. Pressure.

I lectured once to a group of priests and nuns about the sensory experience. "I am holding in my hand," I said, "the most sensual book ever written, illustrated, too, with the most sensual pictures you ever saw." I was holding *The Anatomy and Physiology of the Senses.*

All our beliefs and convictions about the existence of an outside world, the only threads we have that connect our lonely solipsism to other forms of life and energy and consciousness "out there" are based on data registered on our sensory radar and processed by our brains.

Each human being is a spaceship. No, each human being is a galaxy spinning lonely in space, and the only contacts we have with other galaxies (light-years away, really) are the flimsy flickerings on our sense organs.

And what an ontological, epistemological leap of faith it is, really, to believe in the existence of each other! You read this page, light hits your eyes, and your brain sees squiggles of black and white which are words. Do you believe that you are really reading what Timothy Leary wrote? Does this pattern of black and white lines lead you to believe in the existence of a seed-bearing, soul-carrying human being, Timothy Leary, who sat one New Year's Day at a wood-grained desk littered with notes, clippings, books, loose tobacco, coffee cups, ashtrays, looking out a picture window at the silver-gray expanse of the Pacific Ocean, writing these lines?

How can you be sure that Bacon wrote Shakespeare? How can you be sure that those lines were not arranged by a computer which (reacting to a Hooper-rating survey) proceeded to scan and sort quadrillions of pages of past computer writing and rearrange these lines designed to feed back exactly that level of ignorance-superstition-word magic that will comfort and please you? Do you accept your ocular data (this book) that Timothy Leary exists? If you could touch me, smell me, feel my warmth, hear my voice or my smoker's cough, would you be more convinced that I exist?

Common sense convinces us and Dr. Johnson that something exists out there.

But the mystery of knowing remains. And the awesome findings of biochemical neurology do not simplify our understanding of how we know, how we become conscious.

The human brain, we are told, is composed of about ten billion nerve cells, any one of which may connect with as many as 25,000 other nerve cells. The number of interconnections which this adds up to would stagger even an astronomer—and astronomers are used to dealing with astronomical numbers. The number is far greater than all the atoms in the universe. This is why physiologists remain unimpressed by computers. A computer sophisticated enough to handle this number of interconnections would have to be big enough to cover the earth.[12]

Into this matrix floods "about 100 million sensations a second from . . . [the] . . . various senses." And somewhere in that

10-billion-cell galaxy is a tiny solar system of connected neurons which is aware of your social self. Your "ego" is to your brain what the planet earth is to our galaxy with its 100,000 million suns.

B. *The Psychedelic Answer* to the awareness question should now be apparent. There is no answer, only a bleak choice of blind hope or insightful despair.

On the dour side, the attentive, highly conscious person realizes that he is the almost helpless victim of the accidental or deliberate range of light-sound-pressure-chemical energies that impinge on his sensory nerve endings. At one time, when we were trustfully slumbering, a selfish, insane, power-hungry combine of exploitive conspirators suddenly moved in and systematically censored and manipulated what was to hit our eyes, ears, nose, mouth, skin. A well-organized conspiracy to enslave our consciousness. A science fiction horror movie in which our captors decided exactly which energies and sensory stimuli we could encounter. Our 10-billion-cell nervous systems have been monopolized by these ruthless, selfish captors. We walk around on a fake-prop television studio set that our masters have designed—and we play the parts they assign. Using Pavlovian conditioning of reward and punishment, our grim rulers lead us unsuspectingly to do exactly what they wish.

This grim combine which determines the scope and style of our consciousness (for its own benefit) operates through our parents (themselves blind, frightened slaves) and our educational, acculturation institutions.

We have taken leave of our senses. We have been robbed blind. Sensory conditioning has forced us to accept a "reality" which is a comic-tragic farce illusion. We can never rid ourselves of the insanities deeply imprinted during infancy and childhood on our delicate, vulnerable nervous systems. We can never free ourselves completely.

On the bright side, we can obtain a momentary (and even longer) release from the neurological prison. We can come to our senses, turn off the conditioning and experience afresh the hardly bearable ecstasy of direct energy exploding on our nerve endings. We can become seers, hear-oes, smelling tasters in real touch.

The awakening of the senses is the most basic aspect of the psychedelic experience. The open eye, the naked touch, the intensification and vivification of ear and nose and taste. This is the Zen moment of satori, the nature mystic's high, the sudden centering of consciousness on the sense organ, the real-eye-za-tion that this is it! I am eye! I am hear! I knose! I am in contact!

The ability to turn on the senses, to escape the conditioned mind, to throb in harmony with the energies radiating on the sense organs, the skillful control of one's senses, has for thousands of years been the mark of a sage, a holy man, a radiant teacher.

Control of the senses is a basic part of every enduring religious method. Control does not mean repression or closing off. Control means the ability to turn off the mind, ignore the enticing clamor of symbolic seduction and open the senses like flowers, accepting like sunshine the gift of those energies which man's senses are designed to receive.

5. The Ego Question

A. *The Scientific Answer*
Who am I?

Basic question, invariably and eagerly and insistently answered by social institutions. Always for their own benefit. Every religious hierarchy can tell you who you are—Catholic, Protestant, Jew or atheist. Right? And every government agrees you are an American or a Russian or a Turk. Let's see your passport!

And the endless, lesser, monolithic social agencies tell you who you are—occupation, recreation, political affiliation, social class, status, branch of service.

Now comes the new secular state religion—psychology, with its up-to-date answers. The great ego-identity quest. The national personality sweepstakes. The image game.

For the American the question, who am I? is answered totally in terms of artificial social roles. What part do you play in which TV show? And are you good or bad? How is your Hooper rating? Are you popular? Shallow, transient, secular evasion of the physical and metaphysical identity.

Who am I? The perspective on this question comes only when you step off the TV stage set defined by mass-media-social-psychology-adjustment-normality. I exist at every level of energy and every level of consciousness. Who am I? I'm you.

At the atomic level I am a galaxy of nuclear-powered atoms spinning through changing patterns. I am the universe, the center and guardian temple of all energy. I am God of Light. Who am I? I'm you.

At the cellular level I am the entire chain of life. I am the key rung of the DNA ladder, center of the evolutionary process, the current guardian of the seed, the now-eye of the 2-billion-year-old uncoiling serpent. I am God of Life. I'm you.

At the somatic level I am my body—the most intricate, intelligent, complex form of energy structure. The network of my organs and tissues is the last word in cosmic miniaturization, celestial packaging. I am the Resurrection of the Body. I'm you.

At the sensory level I am the divine receiving station, the sacred communications satellite, a two-legged, trembling-tissue, Jodrell Bank radar telescope, dancing, grumbling, sniffing Geiger counter. I am the Darwinian wiretap, a billion sensory microphones picking up vibrations from planetary energy systems. I am the all-time, worldwide retinal ABC, eardrum RCA, International Smell and Tell, the consolidated General Foods taste laboratory. I am God of Common Sense. I'm you.

But there's an added feature. Each generation, I, the timeless God, atom bearer, seed carrier, return in a new, improved, Detroit-model electrical-eye, horseless, carry-all body pushed onto a new social stage set. I am an American. I was an Irish farmer. I was a Celtic minstrel. I was this one and that one. Each time carried onstage blinking, puking, bawling, bewildered by the bizarre novelty of each new drama, untutored in the language of the new script (did she say her name was Mommie?) , unaware of the plot, each time having forgotten my atomic, cellular, somatic, sensory divinity, each time painfully being pushed and hauled into some ludicrous, histrionic consistency known today as my personality, known yesterday as karma.

Thus, I am the undeniably psychological unit. A mind, a box of conditioned Pavlovian reflexes, a social robot, here adjusted, there maladjusted, sometimes good (approved of) sometimes bad (censored). The center of my psychological mandala, the mainspring of my personality, is social conditioning. Reward and punishment. What will the neighbors think? is the beginning and end of modern psychology.

Now, who am I? I'm you. I'm Timothy What's His Name. I am what the *Reader's Digest* likes and dislikes.

This commitment of ego consciousness to the social game is inevitable and cannot be eliminated despite the poignant appeals to drop out. We cannot drop out of society. We can only drop out of social roles and dramas which are unloving, contracting and which distract us from the discovery of our atomic, cellular, somatic and sensory divinity. Spiritual appeals to transcend the ego are vain. Like any other level of consciousness of energy, ego is. Karma is. All we can do is center ego consciousness and see it in proper relationship to the other "I's." The "social ego" is abysmally trivial when compared to the "atomic I," the "DNA I," but that's the glorious humor of the cosmic hide-and-seek. That "social ego" can possess such eccentric, foolish power to camouflage the other divinities that lie beneath our skin.

So let us pray: Almighty Ego, set I free! Almighty Ego, let my I's see!

B. *The Psychedelic Correlates*

Modern psychology, like modern man, does not like to face the sparse, wrinkled-skin facts about human transience. The personality chess game is blown up to compelling importance. How am I doing? Modern education, advertising, indeed the whole culture, is hooked up in a full-time hard-sell campaign to reassure the average person that he is a good Joe, a helluva guy.

Then he takes LSD.

Sensory chaos, somatic inundation, cellular revelation. The plastic-doll nature of social reality and social ego is glaringly obvious. In a word, ego discovers that ego is a fraudulent actor in a fake show. Rubber stamp and tinsel.

Ego discovers that I is atomic, cellular, sensory, somatic and soon to pass on. Ego gets frightened. Panicked. Ego cries for help. Get me a psychiatrist! Help! Get me back to the nice, comforting TV stage.

The impact of LSD is exactly this brutal answer to the question, who is ego? The LSD revelation is the clear perspective. The LSD panic is the terror that ego is lost forever. The LSD ecstasy is the joyful discovery that ego, with its pitiful shams and strivings, is only a fraction of my identity.

6. The Emotional Question

A. *The Scientific Answer.*

What should I move toward? What direction my motion? What should I feel? The emotional and feeling questions.

Here science fails miserably to give us answers because there is little objective data, and the accepted theories of emotional behavior—the psychiatric—are naïve, inadequate, pompously trivial. The best-known theory of emotions, the Freudian, is a hodgepodge of platitude, banality and rabbinical piety.

All that Freud said is that modern man and society are completely dishonest. Society lies to the individual and forces him to lie to himself. Freud called this process of self-deception the unconscious. The unconscious is the hidden. Freud (the lie detector who lied) conscientiously listed the various ways in which man prevaricates and then developed a system of humiliating cross-examination and spirit-breaking brainwashing which forces the rare "successful" patient to give up his favorite pack of lies (which he chose as being the best solution to an impossible situation) and grovelingly to accept the psychoanalyst's system of dishonesty. Have you ever noticed how unbearably "dead" and juiceless psychoanalysts and their patients are? The only cheerful fact about psychoanalysis is that most patients don't get cured and are stubborn enough to preserve their own amateur and original lie in favor of the psychoanalyst's conforming lie.

If anyone has any lingering doubt about the superstitious and barbarian state of psychiatry and psychoanalysis, reflect on this fact. Today, fifty years after Freud, the average mental hospital in the United States is a Kafkaesque, Orwellian, prison camp more terrifying than Dachau because the captors claim to be healers. Two hundred years ago our treatment of the village idiot and nutty old Aunt Agatha was gently utopian compared to the intolerant savagery of the best mental hospital.

So where do we find the scientific answer to the emotional question? Can you really bear to know?

Emotions are the lowest form of consciousness. Emotional actions are the most contracted, narrowing, dangerous form of behavior.

The romantic poetry and fiction of the last 200 years has quite blinded us to the fact that emotions are an active and harmful form of stupor.

Any peasant can tell you that. Beware of emotions. Any child can tell you that. Watch out for the emotional person. He is a lurching lunatic.

Emotions are caused by biochemical secretions in the body to serve during the state of acute emergency. An emotional person is a blind, crazed maniac. Emotions are addictive and narcotic and stupefacient.

Do not trust anyone who comes on emotional.

What are the emotions?

In a book entitled *Interpersonal Diagnosis of Personality,* written when I was a psychologist, I presented classifications of emotions and detailed descriptions of their moderate and extreme manifestations. Emotions are all based on fear. Like an alcoholic or a junkie, the frightened person reaches for his favorite escape into action.

Commanding, competing, punishing, aggressing, rebelling, complaining, abasing, submitting, placating, agreeing, fawning, flattering, giving.

The emotional person cannot think; he cannot perform any

effective game action (except in acts of physical aggression and strength). The emotional person is turned off sensually. His body is a churning robot; he has lost all connection with cellular wisdom or atomic revelation. The person in an emotional state is an inflexible robot gone berserk.

What psychologists call love is emotional greed and self-enhancing gluttony based on fear.

B. *The Psychedelic Correlate*

The only state in which we can learn, harmonize, grow, merge, join, understand is the absence of emotion. This is called bliss or ecstasy, attained through centering the emotions.

Moods such as sorrow and joy accompany emotions. Like a junkie who has just scored or an alcoholic with a bottle in hand, the emotional person feels good when he has scored emotionally, i.e., beaten someone up or been beaten up. Won a competitive victory. Gorged himself on person grabbing.

Conscious love is not an emotion; it is serene merging with yourself, with other people, with other forms of energy. Love cannot exist in an emotional state.

Only the person who has been psychotic or had a deep psychedelic trip can understand what emotions do to the human being.

The great kick of the mystic experience, the exultant, ecstatic hit, is the sudden relief from emotional pressure.

Did you imagine that there could be emotions in heaven? Emotions are closely tied to ego games. Check your emotions at the door to paradise.

Why, then, are emotions built into the human repertoire if they are so painful, demanding and blinding? There is a basic survival purpose. Emotions are the emergency alarms. The organism at the point of death terror goes into a paroxysm of frantic activity. Like a fish flipping blindly out of water. Like a crazed, cornered animal.

There are rare times when emotions are appropriate and relevant. The reflex biochemical spurt. Flight or fight. There are times when emotional bluffs, like the hair rising on a dog's neck, are appropriate. But the sensible animal avoids situations which elicit fear and the accompanying emotion. Your wise animal prefers to relax or to play—using his senses, tuned into his delicious body-organ music, closing his eyes to drift back in cellular memory. Dogs and cats are high all the time—except when bad luck demands emotional measures.

The emotional human being is an evolutionary drug addict continuously and recklessly shooting himself up with adrenalin and other dark ferments. The way to turn off the emotions is to turn on the senses, turn on to your body, turn on to your cellular reincarnation circus, turn on to the electric glow within and engage only in turn-on ego games.

7. The Ultimate Escape Question

A. *The Scientific Answer*
The question is: How does it end?
The answer is: It doesn't.

Ask any scientist (no matter which level of energy he studies), and he'll tell you. It keeps going. At the same beat. On. Off. On. Off.

Atomic. Galaxies flash on and then off.

Cellular. Species flare out and retract.

Somatic. The heart beats and stops. Beats and stops. The lungs inhale and exhale.

Sensory. Light comes in waves of particles hurtling against retinal beaches. High tide, see. Low tide, no see. The neural message dot-dashes along the nerve fibers. Light-dark. Light-dark. Sound waves pile up on the auditory membrane and fall back. Sound-silence. Sound-silence.

There is no form of energy which does not come in the same rhythm. Yin. Yang. In. Out. The galaxy itself and every structure within it is a binary business, an oscillating dance. Start. Stop.

The physicist, the biologist, the physiologist, the neurologist, knows all about the end of the cycle at the level of energy he studies. Every scientist knows that death is exactly symmetrical to birth at every level of energy. Even the sociologists and historians who study the human game structure know that social institutions start and stop.

There is only one level of consciousness that cannot accept the universal on-off switch, and that is the ego. The astronomer can gaze with equanimity at nova explosions and forecast the death of the solar system, but when it comes to his own ego chessboard, there is the illusion of enduring solidity. Ego is unable to learn from the past or to predict the obvious events of the future because of its deep dread of confronting mortality. Ego focuses consciousness on the few immediately neighboring pieces of the game board because ego knows that one glance across the game board or beyond it puts the whole thing in perspective. Where it began and how it will end. Start stop. Off on.

The Buddha's loving parents tried to make sure their son would not consider the four chess pieces that lead off the game board—sickness, age, death, and the magician-guru.

Oriental philosophy points out that every form is an illusion. Maya. Everything at every level of energy is a shuttling series of vibrations as apparently solid as the whirring metal disk made by rotating fan blades. Ego resists this notion and touches the immediate solidity of phenomena. We dislike slowing the motion picture down because the film flickers. Annoying reminder that we view not unbroken continuity but an off-on ribbon of still pictures.

Life is an illusion. There one second, gone the next. Now you see it, now you don't.

Death is equally illusory. Suicide a farce. The desire to escape is exactly as pointless as the desire to hang onto life. How can you clutch onto or escape from a relentless click-clack process that continues despite the mind's interpretation? And despite our "feelings" about it?

But the illusory game goes on. Ego sweats to maintain a tenacious grasp on the ungraspable. And then, in moments of emotional despair, decides to hide, to quit. Hell is the conviction that the game won't stop. Eternal game playing. No exit.

Hell is the idea that the game switch won't turn off. Suicide is the deluded attempt to escape from hell.

Hell is a mistake in judgment. A bum trip idea. The ego's stranglehold on the film projector. Ego is caught in a repetitious loop. Over and over and over. Suicide is the escape from ego. Only ego contemplates escape. Can you imagine an animal killing itself in egocentric pique?

Ego attempts to turn itself off through anesthesia. Unconsciousness. Fast suicide or slow narcosis. Alcohol dulls the mind game and produces emotional stupor. Too much alcohol provides the anesthetic escape. Barbiturates and tranquilizers and sleeping pills are escape tickets bought by the frantic eschatological anethesiologist.

Have you ever talked to an articulate junkie? The appeal of heroin is the void. The warm, soft cocoon of nothingness. Surcease. Easeful death. The vacuum gamble. The game of the junkie is to nod out. To pass over the line into unconsciousness. The last thought of the junkie as he slips away is, have I gone too far this time? Overdose? *Au revoir* or good-bye?

B. *The Psychedelic Correlate*

The deep psychedelic experience is a death-rebirth flip. You turn on to the ancient rhythm, and you become its beat. All right, now! Are you ready? The whole thing is about to click off.

The successful mystic is he who goes with it. Lets it happen. Hello. Good-bye. Hello. Good-bye. Oh, my God! You again!

The bad trip, the LSD panic, is the terrorized reluctance to go with it. Frantic grabbing for the intangible switch. Ego cries, keep it on!

The glory of the psychedelic moment is the victory over life and death won by seeing the oscillating dance of energy and yielding to it.

The age-old appeal of the psychedelic experience is its solution to the problem of escape. The visionary revelation answers the escape question. There is no death. Ecstatic, mirthful relief.

There is nothing to avoid, nothing to escape, nothing to fear. There is just off-on, in-out, start-stop, light-dark, flash-delay.

Death, void, oblivion, is the split-second pause. I accept the on. I accept the off.

It is of interest that the heroin addict and the illuminated Buddha end up at the same place. The void. The junkie is a deeply religious person. The alcoholic is, too. Thus our physicians and psychiatrists have no luck in "curing" addicts. If you see an addict as a social misfit, a civic nuisance who must be rehabilitated, you completely miss the point.

To cure the junkie and the alcoholic, you must humbly admit that he is a more deeply spiritual person than you, and you accept the cosmic validity of his search to transcend the game, and you help him see that blackout drugs are just bad methodology because you just can't keep holding the "off" switch and that the way to reach the void is through psychedelic rather than anesthetic experience.

Drugs Are the Religion of the People—The Only Hope Is Dope

In the preceding pages I have suggested that man can become conscious of each level of energy defined by scientists.

Metaphysics is subjective physics, the psychology of atomic-electronic activity. Metabiology is cellular psychology. Metaphysiology is somatic psychology. The systematic study of internal body states. Metaneurology is sensory physiology, the systematic, introspective study of sense organs. Metapsychology is the study of conditioning by the nervous system that has been conditioned. Your ego unravels its own genesis. Metapsychiatry is the systematic production and control of endocrine states within your own body. Meta-anesthesiology is the systematic production and control of states of unconsciousness within your own body.

Everyone must become his own Einstein, his own Darwin, his own Claude Bernard, his own Penfield, his own Pavlov, his own Freud, his own anesthesiologist.

From the theological standpoint, everyone must discover the seven faces of God within his own body.

This task, which at first glance may seem fantastically utopian, is actually very easy to initiate because there now exist instruments which can move consciousness to any desired level. The laboratory equipment for experimental theology, for internal science, is of course made of the stuff of consciousness itself, made of the same material as the data to be studied. The instruments of systematic religion are chemicals. Drugs. Dope.

If you are serious about your religion, if you really wish to commit yourself to the spiritual quest, you must learn how to use psychochemicals. Drugs are the religion of the twenty-first century. Pursuing the religious life today without using psychedelic drugs is like studying astronomy with the naked eye because that's how they did it in the first century A.D., and besides, telescopes are unnatural.

There Are Specific Drugs to Turn On Each Level of Consciousness

Modern psychopharmacology is written and practiced by scientists who do not take drugs (and who therefore write textbooks about events they have never experienced). Current psychopharmacology is a superstitious form of black magic sponsored and supported by the federal Food and Drug Administration, a government agency about as enlightened as the Spanish Inquisition. Note that the rapidly growing enforcement branch of the FDA uses instruments unknown to Torquemada—guns, wiretaps—in addition to the classic methods of informers and provocateurs. There is thus enormous ignorance about the science of consciousness alteration and a vigorous punitive campaign to prevent its application.

There are specific drugs now easily available which can turn on each level of consciousness. Since Americans are more familiar with and committed to consciousness-contracting drugs, I shall list the better-known psychochemical instruments in reverse order.

7. *The Anesthetic State* is produced by narcotics, barbiturates, and large doses of alcohol. Anyone can reach the void by self-administration of stupefacients. Most Americans know just how to pass out.

6. *The State of Emotional Stupor* is produced by moderate doses of alcohol. Three martinis do nicely.

5. *The State of Ego Consciousness* is enhanced by pep pills, energizers consumed daily by millions of Americans. Pep pills make you feel good. Make you feel active. They change nothing, but they propel you into game motion. Coffee, tea, and Coca-Cola are mild versions.

4. *The State of Sensory Awareness* is produced by any psychedelic drug—LSD, mescaline, psilocybin, MDA, yajé, hashish, Sernyl, DMT—but the specific, direct trigger for turning on the senses is marijuana.

3. *The State of Somatic Awareness* is attained by any psychedelic drugs stronger than marijuana but the specific triggers for cakra consciousness are hashish and MDA.

2. *The Cellular Level of Consciousness* is attained by any of the stronger psychedelics—peyote, LSD, mescaline, psilocybin.

1. *The Atomic-Electronic Level of Consciousness* is produced by the most powerful psychedelics—LSD, STP, DMT.

Try Your Own Experiment

This listing of seven levels of consciousness is based not on revelation or poetic metaphor but on the structure of modern science. We simply assume that there is a different level of consciousness for each major division of science—which, in turn, is based on the major classes of energy manifestation.

The decision as to which drugs turn on which levels of consciousness is empirical, based on thousands of psychedelic experiences. I have personally taken drugs which trigger off each level of consciousness hundreds of times.

But my findings can be easily checked out. Any reader can initiate experiments of his own with easily available chemicals.

Turn on a tape recorder during your next cocktail party. Notice how rational ego-game playing deteriorates and the emotional level rises in exact proportion to the amount of booze consumed. You have moved consciousness from level 5 to level 6.

Next, turn on your tape recorder during a pot party. Notice how the emotional level drops, serenity increases. Observe the intensified attention to sensory energy. The relaxation of game tension. You have moved consciousness from level 5 to level 4.

If you are a diligent experimental theologian, you may wish to see if you can take the fantastic voyage down your body or down into time, using the appropriate chemical instruments. Psychedelic yoga is not a mysterious, arcane specialty reserved for Ph.D.'s and a scientific elite. Anyone who is curious about the nature of God and reality can perform the experiments. Indeed, millions of Americans have done just this in the last few years.

The Seven Religious Yogas

The psychedelic experience, far from being new, is man's oldest and most classic adventure into meaning. Every religion in world history was founded on the basis of some flipped-out visionary trip.

Religion is the systematic attempt at focusing man's consciousness. Comparative religion should concern itself less with the exoteric and academic differences and more with studying the different levels of consciousness turned on by each religion.

We see that there are seven approaches employed by the great world religions.

Seven dialects of God

1. *Buddhism* attempts to transcend life and cellular manifestations and to strive toward the white light of the void, the unitary atomic-electronic flash beyond form.

2. *Hinduism* is a vegetative jungle of reincarnation imagery. Clearly cellular. Evolutionary. Genetic.

3. *Tantra* (Tibetan, Bengali) focuses on somatic energy (Kundalini) and *cakra* consciousness.

4. *Zen, Hasidic Judaism, Sufism, and early Christianity* used methods for centering sensual energy.

5. *Protestantism and Talmudic Judaism* are the classic ego religions. Logic, hard work and Main Street practicality will get you to heaven.

6. *Middle-class Catholicism and devil-oriented fundamentalist sects* are based on the arousal of emotion—fear.

7. *Suicide and death cults*

Different Sciences Study Different Basic Questions

Each of the seven basic questions faced by man has been studied for thousands of years by thoughtful individuals and by institutions, disciplines and professions. In the last 60 years, physical and biological scientists have pretty well agreed on a systematic and unified perspective of the wide range of energy processes and structures. A remarkably efficient classification of subject matter and a civilized, tolerant division of labor have developed.

Scientists generally agree that there are definable levels of energy and, what is most important for harmonious collaboration, agree on the relations of the different levels of energy. The physicist knows that he studies a different phenomenon than the behavioral psychologist. Electrons are different from recorded emotions. Both the physicist and psychologist recognize that atomic processes are basic to and underlie all physiological and psychological activities. A hierarchy of sciences exists, based not on bureaucratic or political factors but on the nature of the level of energy studied. The physicist studies processes which are billions of times smaller (and larger) than those of the psychologist, processes which are billions of times faster and older than human psychological processes. Electrons were spun off the sun billions of years before man's adrenalin glands propelled him to flight.

Each Level of Energy Requires Its Own Methods and Language

Among human beings (members of a species best known for its competitive belligerence and murderous envy), physical and biological scientists are relatively immune to fraternal homicide. Biologists don't war against physicists. An American biologist might war against members of another species, or another nationality or religion. An American bacteriologist might develop a germ used to destroy Vietnamese people, but he does not war against other biologists about biological issues. Indeed, American and Soviet scientists collaborate even during times of political warfare.

The ability of scientists to communicate, teach each other, help each other in spite of racial and national differences is due to the fact that they share an effective, precise language system.

When Johnson and Ho say, "Peace," they use the word quite differently. When Pope Paul and a Buddhist monk say, "God," who knows what they mean?

When a chemist writes a formula, all chemists know what he means. And all physicists know specifically or vaguely how the chemist's molecular formula relates to atomic processes.

The disciplines of neurology, psychology and psychiatry, however, have not yet reached a scientific state. No satisfactory language system exists in their fields. Neurologists quarrel with psychiatrists about the causes of mental illness. Psychologists cannot tell us how man learns or forgets. Enormous priesthoods have developed in these three fields which jockey for power, funds, prestige but which fail to provide answers or even to define problems.

The entire study of consciousness, the religious experience itself, remains in a state of medieval ignorance and superstition. There is no language for describing states of awareness. Religious scholars and theologians quarrel, not just about moral fads and ritual paraphernalia but, more basically, about the answers to the seven basic questions.

The humanistic sciences—neurology, psychology, psychiatry, psychopharmacology and the study of consciousness (which I call religion) —require a systematic language which will allow men to distinguish which levels of energy and consciousness they deal with.

It is rather unfortunate that Western man developed a language of physics and chemistry and a highly efficient engineering based on physical-chemical experimentation long before he developed understanding and control of his own sense organs and neurological conditioning. Thus we now have a situation where blind, irrational, technical robots (who understand neither their makeup nor the purpose of life) are in control of powerful and dangerous energies.

A conversation with Alan Watts:

Leary: Alan, what is the purpose of life?

Watts: That is the question!

Leary: What do you mean?

Watts: The purpose of life is to ask the question, what is the purpose of life? is to ask the question, what is the purpose of life?

The only purpose of life is the religious quest, the religious question. But you must be careful how you put the question because the level at which you ask is the level at which you will be answered.

I have suggested seven levels of energy and consciousness which are based on the anatomy or structure of the human body and its constituent parts—neurological, somatic, cellular, molecular. The religions of the future must be based on these seven scientific questions. A science of consciousness must be based on those different levels which center on the body and the biochemicals (i.e., drugs) which alter consciousness.

Dramatic changes in our child-rearing and educational practices, politics, communications will occur as man grasps this notion of the levels of consciousness and their alteration.

Table 1 presents a highly simplified summary of the seven levels of consciousness and their implications for science, religion, art and drug taking.

TABLE 1

The seven levels of energy consciousness, the drugs which induce them and the sciences and religions which study each level.

Level of Energy Consciousness	Directing Intelligence Communication Center	Communication Structure	Science	Drug to produce this level	Religious centering on this level	Religion metaphor	Art using this level of energy	Sacramental method
1. Atomic	Nucleus of atom	Electron	Physics Astrophysics	LSD* STP	Buddhism	White Light	Psychedelic light electronic music	Until psychedelics spontaneous
2. Cellular	DNA	RNA	Biology Biochemistry	Peyote Psilocybin Yage	Hinduism	Reincarnation	Hindu art	Prolonged fasting
3. Somatic	Autonomic nerve plexes	Organs of body	Physiology	MDA Hashish	Tantra	Cakras Kundalini	Bosch	Sensory deprivation
4. Sensory	Brain	Sense organs	Neurology	Marijuana	Zen, Sufism, early Christianity, Hasidic	Satori	Sensory art	Incense Dance Music Chanting, etc.
5. Mental-Social	Mind imprint plus conditioning	Social behavior	Psychology	Pep pills	Judaism Protestantism Judaism	Christ Messiah	Reproductive art	Sermons
6. Emotional stupor	Endocrine centers	Emotional behavior	Psychiatry	Alcohol	Catholicism Fundamentalism	Devil	Propaganda	Superstitious ritual
7. Void			Anesthesiology	Narcotics Poisons	Death cults	Black Void		Suicide Ritual murder

* While many drugs induce awareness at more than one level (for example hashish turns on at levels 4 and 5), only LSD can move consciousness to all seven levels (often at the same instant).

Science as Ecstatic Kick

When we read about the current findings of the energy sciences such as those I have just reviewed, how can our reaction be other than reverent awe at the grandeur of these observations, at the staggering complexity of the design, the speed, the scope? Ecstatic humility before such power and intelligence. Indeed, what a small, secular concept—intelligence—to describe that infinitude of harmonious complexity! How impoverished our vocabulary and how narrow our imagination!

Of course, the findings of the pure sciences *do not* produce the religious reaction we should expect. We are satiated with secular statistics, dazed into robot dullness by the enormity of facts which we are not educated to comprehend. Although the findings of physics, genetics, paleontology and neurology have tremendous relevance to our life, they are of less interest than a fall in the stock market or the status of the pennant race.

The message is dimly grasped hypothetically, rationally, but never experienced, felt, known. But there can be that staggering, intellectual-game ecstasy which comes when you begin to sense the complexity of the plan. To pull back the veil and see for a second a fragment of the energy dance, the life power. How can you appreciate the divine unless you comprehend the smallest part of the fantastic design? To experience (it's always for a moment) the answers to the seven basic spiritual questions is to me the peak of the religious-scientific quest.

But how can our ill-prepared nervous systems grasp the message? Certainly the average man cannot master the conceptual, mathematical bead game of the physics graduate student. Must his experiential contact with the divine process come in watered-down symbols, sermons, hymns, robot rituals, religious calendar art, moral-behavior sanctions eventually secular in their aim? Fortunately the great plan has produced a happy answer and has endowed every human being with the equipment to comprehend, to know, to experience directly, incontrovertibly. It's there in that network of 10 billion cells, the number of whose interconnections "is far greater than all the atoms in the universe."

If you can, for the moment, throw off the grip of your learned mind, your conditioning, and experience the message contained in the 10-billion-tube computer which you carry behind your forehead, you would know the awe-full truth. Our research suggests that even the uneducated layman can experience directly what is slowly deduced by scientists—for example, physicists, whose heavy, conceptual minds lumber along at three concepts a second, attempting to fathom the speed-of-light processes which their beautiful machines record and which their beautiful symbols portray.

But the brakes can be released. Our recent studies support the hypothesis that psychedelic foods and drugs, ingested by prepared subjects in a serious, sacred, supportive atmosphere, can put the subject in perceptual touch with other levels of energy exchanges. Remember the data—the Good Friday study, the Savage study, the 200 religious professionals, 40 to 90 percent telling us they experienced "a greater awareness of God or a higher power or an ultimate reality."

The Language of Ecstasy

But to what do these LSD subjects refer when they report spiritual reactions? Do they obtain specific illuminations into the seven basic questions, or are their responses simply awe and wonder at the experienced novelty? Even if the latter were the case, could it not support the religious application of the psychedelic substances and simply underline the need for more sophisticated religious language coordinated with the scientific data? But there is some evidence, phenomenological but yet haunting, that the spiritual insights accompanying the psychedelic experience might be subjective accounts of the objective findings of astronomy, physics, biochemistry, and neurology.

Now the neurological and pharmacological explanations of

an LSD vision are still far from being understood. We know almost nothing about the physiology of consciousness and the body-cortex interaction. We cannot assert that LSD subjects are directly experiencing what particle physicists and biochemists measure, but the evidence about the detailed complexity of the genetic code and the astonishing design of intracellular communication should caution us against labeling experiences outside of our current tribal clichés as "psychotic" or abnormal. For 3,000 years our greatest prophets and philosophers have been telling us to look within, and today our scientific data are supporting that advice with a humiliating finality. The limits of introspective awareness may well be submicroscopic, cellular, molecular and even nuclear. We only see, after all, what we are trained and predisposed to see. One of our current research projects involves teaching subjects to recognize internal physical processes much as we train a beginning biology student to recognize events viewed through his microscope.

No matter how parsimonious our explanations, we must accept the fact that LSD subjects do claim to experience revelations into the basic questions and do attribute life change to their visions.

We are, of course, at the very beginning of our research into these implications. A new experiential language and perhaps even new metaphors for the great plan will develop. We have been working on this project for the past six years, writing manuals which train subjects to recognize energy processes, teaching subjects to communicate via a machine we call the experiential typewriter and with movies of microbiological processes. And we have continued to pose the questions to religious and philosophic groups: What do you think? Are these biochemical visions religious?

Before you answer, remember that God (however you define the higher power) produced that wonderful molecule, that extraordinarily powerful organic substance we call LSD, just as surely as He created the rose, or the sun, or the complex cluster of molecules you insist on calling your "self."

Professional Priests and Theologians Avoid the Religious Experience

Among the many harassing complications of our research into religious experience has been the fact that few people, even some theological professionals, have much conception of what a religious experience really is. Few have any idea how the divine process presents itself. If asked, they tend to become embarrassed, intellectual, evasive. The adored cartoonists of the Renaissance portray the ultimate power as a dove, or a flaming bush, or as a man—venerable, with a white beard, or on a cross, or as a baby, or a sage seated in the full lotus position. Are these not limiting incarnations, temporary housings, of the great energy process?

In the fall of 1962, a minister and his wife, as part of a courageous and dedicated pursuit of illumination, took a psychedelic biochemical called dimethyltriptamine. This wondrous alkaloid (which closely approximates serotonin, the natural "lubricant" of our higher nervous system) produces an intense psychedelic effect. In twenty-five minutes (about the duration of the average sermon) you are whirled through the energy dance, the cosmic process, at the highest psychedelic speed. The twenty-five minutes are sensed as lasting for a second and for a billion-year Kalpa. After the session, the minister complained that the experience, although shattering and revelatory, was disappointing because it was "content-free"—so physical, so unfamiliar, so scientific, like being beamed through microscopic panoramas, like being oscillated through cellular functions at radar acceleration. Well, what do you expect? If God were to take you on a visit through His "workshop," do you think you'd walk or go by bus? Do you really think it would be a stroll through a celestial Madame Tussaud waxworks? Dear friends, the *divine product* is evident in every macroscopic form, in every secular event. The divine product we can see. But the *divine process* operates in time dimensions which are far beyond our routine, secular, space-time limits. Wave vibrations, energy dance, cellular transactions. Our science describes this logically. Our brains may be capable of dealing with these processes experientially.

So here we are. The great process has placed in our hands a key to this direct visionary world. Is it hard for us to accept that the key might be an organic molecule and not a new myth or a new word?

The Politics of Revelation

And where do we go? There are in the United States today several million persons who have experienced what I have attempted to describe—a psychedelic, religious revelation. There are, I would estimate, several million equally thoughtful people who have heard the joyous tidings and who are waiting patiently but determinedly for the prohibition to end.

There is, of course, the expected opposition. The classic conflict of the religious drama—always changing, always the same. The doctrine (which was originally someone's experience) now threatened by the *new* experience. This time the administrators have assigned the inquisitorial role to the psychiatrists, whose proprietary claims to a revealed understanding of the mind and whose antagonism to consciousness expansion are well known to you.

The clamor over psychedelic drugs is now reaching full crescendo. You have heard rumors and you have read the press assaults and the slick-magazine attacks-by-innuendo. As sophisticated adults, you have perhaps begun to wonder: why the hysterical outcry? As scientists, you are beginning to ask: where is the evidence? As educated men with an eye for history, you are, I trust, beginning to suspect that we've been through this many times before.

In the current hassle over psychedelic plants and drugs, you are witnessing a good, old-fashioned, traditional, religious controversy. On the one side the psychedelic visionaries, somewhat uncertain about the validity of their revelations, embarrassedly speaking in new tongues (there never is, you know, the satisfaction of a sound, right academic language for the new vision of the divine), harassed by the knowledge of their own human frailty, surrounded by the inevitable legion of eccentric would-be followers looking for a new panacea, always in grave doubt about their own motivation—hero? martyr? crank? crackpot?—always on the verge of losing their material achievements—job, reputation, long-suffering wife, conventional friends, parental approval—always under the fire of the power holders. And on the other side the establishment (the administrators, the police, the fund-granting foundations, the job givers) pronouncing their familiar lines in the drama: "Danger! Madness! Unsound! Intellectual corruption of youth! Irreparable damage! Cultism!" The issue of chemical expansion of consciousness is hard upon us. During the last few years, every avenue of propaganda has barraged you with the arguments. You can hardly escape it. You are going to be pressed for a position. Internal freedom is becoming a major religious and civil rights controversy.

How can you decide? How can you judge? Well, it's really quite simple. Whenever you hear anyone sounding off on internal freedom and consciousness-expanding foods and drugs—whether pro or con—check out these questions:

1. Is your expert talking from direct experience, or simply repeating clichés? Theologians and intellectuals often deprecate "experience" in favor of fact and concept. This classic debate is falsely labeled. Most often it becomes a case of "experience" versus "inexperience."

2. Do his words spring from a spiritual or from a mundane point of view? Is he motivated by a dedicated quest for answers to basic questions, or is he protecting his own social-psychological position, his own game investment? Is he struggling toward sainthood, or is he maintaining his status as a hard-boiled scientist or hard-boiled cop?

3. How would his argument sound if it were heard in a different culture (for example, in an African jungle hut, a *ghat* on the Ganges, or on another planet inhabited by a form of life superior to ours) or in a different time (for example, in Periclean Athens, or in a Tibetan monastery, or in a bull session led

by any one of the great religious leaders—founders—messiahs) ? Or how would it sound to other species of life on our planet today—to the dolphins, to the consciousness of a redwood tree? In other words, try to break out of your usual tribal game set and listen with the ears of another one of God's creatures.

4. How would the debate sound to you if you were fatally diseased with a week to live, and thus less committed to mundane issues? Our research group receives many requests a week for consciousness-expanding experiences, and some of these come from terminal patients.[13]

5. Is the point of view one which opens up or closes down? Are you being urged to explore, experience, gamble out of spiritual faith, join someone who shares your cosmic ignorance on a collaborative voyage of discovery? Or are you being pressured to close off, protect your gains, play it safe, accept the authoritative voice of someone who knows best?

6. When we speak, we say little about the subject matter and disclose mainly the state of our own mind. Does your psychedelic expert use terms which are positive, pro-life, spiritual, inspiring, opening, based on faith in the future, faith in your potential, or does he betray a mind obsessed by danger, material concern, by imaginary terrors, administrative caution or essential distrust in your potential? Dear friends, there is nothing in life to fear; no spiritual game can be lost.

7. If he is against what he calls "artificial methods of illumination," ask him what constitutes the natural. Words? Rituals? Tribal customs? Alkaloids? Psychedelic vegetables?

8. If he is against biochemical assistance, where does he draw the line? Does he use nicotine? alcohol? penicillin? vitamins? conventional sacramental substances?

9. If your advisor is against LSD, what is he for? If he forbids you the psychedelic key to revelation, what does he offer you instead?

REFERENCES

[1] Walter N. Pahnke, *Drugs and Mysticism: An Analysis of the Relationship between Psychedelic Drugs and the Mystical Consciousness.* A thesis

presented to the Committee on Higher Degrees in History and Philosophy of Religion, in partial fulfillment of the requirements for the degree of doctor of philosophy, Harvard University, Cambridge, Massachusetts, June 1963.

[2] "The Subjective After-Effects of Psychedelic Experiences: A Summary of Four Recent Questionnaire Studies," *Psychedelic Review*, Vol. I, No. I (June 1963), pp. 18–26.

[3] T. Leary, G. H. Litwin, and R. Metzner, "Reactions to Psilocybin Administered in a Supportive Environment," *Journal of Nervous and Mental Disease*, Vol. 137, No. 6 (December 1963), pp. 561–73.

[4] C. Savage, W. W. Harman, and J. Fadiman, "A Follow-up Note on the Psychedelic Experience." Paper delivered at a meeting of the American Psychiatric Association. St. Louis, Missouri, May 1963.

[5] K. S. Ditman, M. Haymon, and J. R. S. Whittlesey, "Nature and Frequency of Claims Following LSD," *Journal of Nervous and Mental Disease*, Vol. 134 (1962), pp. 346–52.

[6] W. H. McGlothlin, *Long-Lasting Effects of LSD on Certain Attitudes in Normals: An Experimental Proposal*. Privately printed, The Rand Corporation, Santa Monica, California, June 1962, p. 56. Cf. W. H. McGlothlin, S. Cohen, and M. S. McGlothlin, *Short-Term Effects of LSD on Anxiety, Attitudes, and Performance. Ibid.*, June 1963, p. 15.

[7] A continuing present-day instance is the case of members of the Native American Church, a duly constituted and recognized religious denomination numbering almost a quarter of a million adherents. A good popular account of their situation is presented in "Peyote," by A. Stump, in *Saga*, Vol. 26, No. 3 (June 1963), pp. 46–49, 81–83. Cf. the Supreme Court's decision, Oliver v. Udall, 306 F2d 819 (1962). The most recently proposed legislation against peyote is seen in the *Congressional Record* (House) for December 13, 1963. W. La Barre's famous book, *The Peyote Cult*, was reprinted in an enlarged edition in August 1964 by the Shoe String Press (Hamden, Connecticut) and brings the entire discussion up to date. For a good general statement in another area of research, see "The Hallucinogenic Drugs," by Barron, Jarvik, and Bunnell, *Scientific American*, Vol. 210, No. 4 (April 1964), pp. 29–37.

[8] R. C. Zaehner, *At Sundry Times*, London: Faber & Faber, 1958, p. 57. An essay in the comparison of religions.

[9] H. Woltereck, *What Science Knows About Life*, New York: Association Press, 1963.

[10] G. Schenk, *The History of Man*, New York: Chilton, 1961, pp. 56–57.

[11] *Ibid.*, p. 238.

[12] R. Campbell, "The Circuits of the Senses," in a series on "The Human Body" (Part IV), *Life*, Vol. 54, No. 27 (June 27, 1963), pp. 64–76b.

[13] The medical press has recently reported on the analgesic use of LSD with terminal cancer patients. Cf. *Medical World News* (August 30, 1963), *Medical Tribune* (April 8, 1963), and *Journal of the American Medical Association* (January 4, 1964).

2

What to Do When the Vietcong Drop LSD in Our Water Supply*

Psychiatric Panic

An article by Dr. E. James Lieberman entitled "Psycho-Chemicals as Weapons," published in the January 1962 *Bulletin of Atomic Science,* could lead to serious confusion in the minds of a credulous public and a credulous military. The author seems to be moved by admirable democratic sentiments, but he has mixed together an astonishing combination of psychiatric folklore and chemical warfare fantasy. The results are misleading.

The so-called psychotropic weapons deplored in this article are lysergic acid diethylamide (LSD), mescaline (the synthetic of the "divine peyote cactus"), and psilocybin (the synthetic of the sacred mushroom of Mexico). The author, a psychiatrist, warns that "catastrophic damage that would be neither reversible nor humane" might follow the ingestion of these drugs.

Dr. Lieberman has presented one of the many sharply divergent viewpoints about the interpretation and application of these drugs. Many psychiatrists believe that LSD, mescaline and psilocybin produce psychiatric symptoms—anxiety, depression, detachment, confusion, suspicion, psychosis. Many other investigators have come to the conclusion that these symptoms exist

---

* This article was written with the help of George Litwin, Michael Hollingshead, Gunther Weil and Richard Alpert, and was first published in the *Bulletin of Atomic Science,* May 1962.

mainly in the mind and eye of the psychiatrist and that consciousness-expanding chemicals, far from being dangerous weapons, may produce dramatic changes in personality leading to unprecedented peace, sanity and happiness.

Perhaps it depends on what you are trained to look for. Most psychiatrists who have experimented with such consciousness-affecting drugs report danger. Most nonpsychiatrists see these drugs as great benefactors of mankind. Included in the latter group are Albert Hoffman, the brilliant biochemist who first synthesized LSD and psilocybin; Alan Watts, author and philosopher; Robert S. de Ropp, biochemist; Aldous Huxley, novelist and philosopher; and the great American psychologist and philosopher William James. Also included among those who hail the humanistic promise of consciousness-expanding drugs are a few psychiatrists who have seen beyond psychopathology to the adaptive potential of the human brain.

What Are Psychedelic Drugs?

So much for the controversial. Research and not words will resolve these issues. But let us look next at the secure knowledge which exists concerning mescaline, LSD, and psilocybin. What are these substances? Sacramental foods? Devilish weapons? Wonder medicines? It is easier to say what they are not. They are not addictive, nor sedative, nor intoxicating. There is no evidence for any lasting and very few transient physical effects. Everyone agrees on one factor—they dramatically alter consciousness and expand awareness.

There is a second generally shared conclusion. Set and suggestibility, expectation and emotional atmosphere account for almost all of the specificity of reaction. If the drug giver is supportive, open, relaxed, then the results will usually be positive, educational, dramatically insightful. If, on the other hand, the drug giver is secretive, depersonalized, himself fearful of the drug, then the reactions will probably be anxious and unpleasant.

As members of a research project studying the effects and application of consciousness-expanding drugs, we have had the opportunity of observing the behavioral and phenomenological reactions of thousands of subjects. A glance at some of our results suggests that the military applications of consciousness-expanding drugs may be limited. To date, 91 percent of the Americans who have participated in our research report pleasant, inspirational experiences. Even with no attempt to be therapeutic and with only one ingestion, over 60 percent of our subjects report subsequent life changes for the better.

During 1962–63 we used these drugs for rehabilitation purposes in a maximum-security prison. During more than 100 individual ingestions by hardened criminals, we witnessed dramatic insight and behavior-change reactions.

Beware Fear and Ignorance

Like any product of our advanced technology, the consciousness-expanding drugs can be used to manipulate, dominate, frighten or benefit mankind. A hypodermic syringe of LSD or Salk vaccine in the hands of an enemy can become a frightening weapon. However, the greatest enemies of mankind are ignorance and fear. In the hands of the unfriendly, these weapons can paralyze and destroy.

What are the protections? Accurate information openly shared and calm, courageous response to the evidence. Psychiatrists and physicians on whom Dr. Lieberman calls for rescue from danger, perhaps imaginary, can help to the extent they are collaborative, open, fearless with their fellow men. If the American people are frightened by psychopathological obsessions and psychiatric superstitions and ill-kept chemical warfare secrets, they can be hurt. We are least vulnerable and strongest when we are well-informed. Facts are the defense against any weapon, and particularly the psychological weapons of fear and helplessness.

Be Prepared

The facts about consciousness-expanding substances are not all in yet, but some things are clear. Physiologically these substances act mainly on the brain stem, disinhibiting certain regulating, selecting, screening and controlling mechanisms that constantly guide our perception and thinking. The higher, conscious centers are free temporarily from these artificial restrictions. Behaviorally the main effect of these substances is relaxation. Most of our subjects are very happy just to sit and enjoy the world. There is much less talking, much less superficial movement or conversation. Let us be clear; almost all of our subjects could function very adequately if called on. They choose to relax. Psychologically these amazing substances expand your awareness, open your mind. The kaleidoscopic and complex world that has always been there, the powerful sensations from every part of your body and the unusual connections of thoughts and feelings that are normally ignored come dramatically into consciousness.

Of course these experiences can be frightening. If you are not prepared, if you do not know what is happening to you and your brain, if you are struggling to maintain complete verbal control over your senses and your awareness, you will certainly be frightened. But if you are prepared, if you know what kind of a chemical you have taken and what to expect (which most subjects participating in psychiatric research with these substances do not), if you do relax, then the experience can be wonderful, enlightening, and life-changing. If an enemy drops LSD in the water supply and if you are accurately informed and prepared, then you have two choices. If you have the time and inclination, you should sit back and enjoy the most exciting educational experience of your life (you might be forever grateful to the saboteur). If you don't have the time or inclination for this pleasant and insightful experience, then swallow a tranquilizer, and you'll be back to the prosaic reality. Tomorrow the drugs and the counterdrugs may be different, but the prescription is the same.

Turn On the Pentagon

If an enemy introduced a consciousness-expanding drug into a military command center, our leaders—if they are accurately informed and experienced about the potentials of expanded awareness—might find that men in certain key positions could function better. In fact, we must assume that these substances are now being used by our space agency for the preparation of astronauts, who will certainly undergo altered states of consciousness in space exploration.

Your brain is your own. Intelligent, open collaboration can expand your mind—with words and with drugs. Only ignorance and misinformation can allow someone else to control it—with their own words or with their drugs or with their imaginary fears.

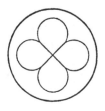

SEAL OF THE LEAGUE

3

The Fifth Freedom—
The Right to Get High*

Expansion and Contraction Is the Rhythm of the Universe

The tension between the flowing process and the fixed structure. Let go! Pull back! Let go! Pull back!

Inorganic processes: The expanding gaseous cloud whirls into temporary patterned structures. The structures always changing, hurtling toward eventual entropy. Let go. Pull back.

Organic processes: Watery, electro-biochemical globules cluster into cells. Cells cluster into temporary hardened forms (vegetative or animal), themselves always changing, eventually returning to the entropic. Let go. Pull back.

Social processes: The free, expansive vision is molded into the institutional. Hardly has the institutional mortar set before there is a new cortical upheaval, an explosive, often ecstatic or prophetic revelation. The prophet is promptly jailed. A hundred years later his followers are jailing the next visionary.

The Ancient Game: Visionary vs. Cop

One is led naïvely to exclaim: Will man never learn the lesson of cyclical process? Must we continue to jail, execute, exile our ecstatic visionaries and then enshrine them as tomorrow's heroes?

---

* Written with the help of my friend Richard Alpert and first published in the *Harvard Review*, Vol. I, No. 4, Summer 1963.

Naïve questions, which fail to appreciate the necessary tension of the expansion-contraction play. Membrane contracts. Life force bursts membrane. Establishment controls vision. Vision bursts establishment. Let go. Pull back.

The expansion process in physics and biology is described in evolutionary terms. Let go.

The expansion process in human affairs is defined in terms of the word "freedom." Let go.

We measure social evolution in terms of increased freedom— external or internal. Freedom to step out of the tribal game and move to construct a new social form. Freedom to move in space. Freedom to experience. Freedom to explore. Freedom to get high. Freedom to let go.

The Hippy vs. Square Quarrel Is a Bore

Society needs conscientious, dogmatic priest-scholars to provide structure—the intellectual muscle, bone and skin to keep things together. The university is the establishment's apparatus for training consciousness contractors. The intellectual ministry of defense. Defense against vision. This statement is not pejorative but a fact about evolutionary function. We need stability. But we need expansion, too. We need the far-out visionary as well as the up-tight academic council which sits in learned judgment on Socrates, Galileo, Bacon, Columbus, Thoreau. The protagonists in these dramas are neither good nor evil. No villains, no heroes. They just are. What will be the next step in biological and social evolution? Here are two clues. (1) You are more likely to find the evolutionary agents closer to jail than to the professor's chair. (2) Look to that social freedom most abused, most magically, irrationally feared by society. Exactly that freedom which *you*, the intellectual, the liberal, would deny to others. Good. Now you are getting close.

The administration always recognizes intuitively the next evolutionary step that will leave it behind. To cast this drama in terms of saints and Pharisees is entertaining, but outmoded.

The drama is genetic. Neurophysiological.

So spare us, please, the adolescent heroics of Beethoven and Shakespeare.

The Next Lunge Forward

Where, then, will the next evolutionary step occur? Within the human cortex. We *know*, yes we *know*, that science has produced methods for dramatically altering and expanding human awareness and potentialities. The uncharted realm lies behind your own forehead. Internal geography. Internal politics. Internal control. Internal freedom.

The nervous system can be changed, integrated, recircuited, expanded in its function. These possibilities naturally threaten every branch of the establishment. The dangers of external change appear to frighten us less than the peril of internal change. LSD is more frightening than the bomb!

We are, in a real sense, prisoners of the cognitive concepts and intellectual strategies which are passed on from generation to generation. The cognitive continuity of history. And the stuff of it is words. Our current reliance upon substantive and "closing-off" concepts will be the amused wonder of coming generations. We must entertain nonverbal methods of communication if we are to free our nervous system from the tyranny of the stifling simplicity of words.

Cortical Vitamins

Biochemical methods of increasing cortical efficiency. Biochemicals in the human body, in plants, and in drugs. There exist in nature hundreds of botanical species with psychedelic ("mind-opening") powers. There exists around the indole circle a wide variety of psychedelic compounds. Cortical vitamins.

The existence of these substances has been known for thousands of years but has been maintained as a well-guarded secret. The scarcity of botanical supply. Today the mind-opening substances (e.g., mescaline, LSD, psilocybin) are available for the first time in limitless, mass-produced quantities. What a threat! What a challenge! What a widespread menace!

The danger, of course, is not physical. As of 1968 there was no evidence that LSD causes pathological changes in the brain, the body, or the genetic material. The anti-LSD warnings of American scientists are out-and-out hoax. Government science, like Hitler's race experiments and Soviet genetics.

Turn On or Bail Out

The danger of LSD is not physical or psychological, but social-political. Make no mistake: the effect of consciousness-expanding drugs will be to transform our concepts of human nature, human potentialities, existence. The game is about to be changed, ladies and gentlemen. Man is about to make use of that fabulous electrical network he carries around in his skull. Present social establishments had better be prepared for the change. Our favorite concepts are standing in the way of a flood tide 2 billion years building up. The verbal dam is collapsing. Head for the hills, or prepare your intellectual craft to flow with the current.

The Visionary Automobile

Let's try a metaphor. The social situation in respect to psyche-delic drugs is very similar to that faced 60 years ago by those crackpot visionaries who were playing around with the horseless carriage. Of course the automobile is external child's play compared to the unleashing of cortical energy, but the social dilemma is similar.

The claim was made in 1900 that the motor carriage, accelerated to speeds several times that of the horse-drawn vehicle, would revolutionize society. Impossible to conceptualize because in 1900 we possessed no concepts for these possibilities. First of all, we object to the dangers: high speeds will snap nervous minds, gas fumes are fatal, the noise will prevent cows from giving milk, horses will run away, criminals will exploit the automobile.

Then the puritanical objection: people will use cars for pleasure, for kicks.

Then we question the utility: what can we do with speedy carriages? There are no men to repair them. There are no roads, few bridges. There are no skilled operators. The supply of fuel is small. Who will sell you gas?

Then we raise the problem of control: who should be allowed to own and operate these powerful and dangerous instruments? Perhaps they should be restricted to the government elite, to the military, to the medical profession.

But why do we want cars, anyway? What is wrong with the good old buggy? What will happen to coachmen, blacksmiths, carriage makers?

The automotive visionary of 1900 could have pointed out that his skeptical opponent had no concepts, no social structures to implement these possibilities. Remember, if one talks about experiences and prospects for which the listener has no concepts, then he is defined (at best) as a mystic. Our automotive mystic sixty years ago would have asserted the need for a new language, new social forms, and would have predicted that our largest national industry would inevitably develop out of this vision.

Can you imagine a language without such words as *convertible, tudor sedan, General Motors, U.A.W., Standard Oil, superhighway, parking ticket, traffic court?* These most commonplace terms in our present culture were mystical images three generations ago.

Who Controls the Instruments of Freedom?

In totalitarian states the use and control of instruments for external freedom—the automobile, the private airplane—are reserved for the government bureaucracy and the professional elite. Even in democracies the traditional means for expanding or contracting consciousness (internal freedom), such as the printing press, radio transmitter, motion picture, are restricted by law and remain under government control.

Now consider psychedelic drugs. No language to describe the experience. No trained operators to guide the trip. Lots of blacksmiths whose monopoly is threatened. A few people who do see an inevitable development of a new language, a transfiguration of every one of our social forms. And these few, of course, the ones who have taken the internal voyage.

It is possible that in 20 years our psychological and experiential language (pitifully small in English) will have multiplied to cover realms of experience and forms of thinking now unknown. In 20 years every social institution will have been transformed by the new insights provided by consciousness-expanding experiences. Many new social institutions will have developed to handle the expressions of the potentiated nervous system.

The Fifth Freedom

The political issue involves control: "automobile" means that the free citizen moves *his* own car in external space. Internal automobile. Auto-administration. The freedom and control of one's experiential machinery. Licensing will be necessary. You must be trained to operate. You must demonstrate your proficiency to handle consciousness-expanding drugs without danger to yourself or the public. The fifth freedom—the freedom to expand your own consciousness—cannot be denied without due cause.

A final hint to those who have ears to hear. The open cortex produces an ecstatic state. The nervous system operating free of learned abstraction is a completely adequate, completely efficient, ecstatic organ. To deny this is to rank man's learned concepts above 2 billion years' endowment. An irreverent act. Trust your inherent machinery. Be entertained by the social game you play. Remember, man's natural state is ecstatic wonder, ecstatic intuition, ecstatic, accurate movement. Don't settle for less.

4

Ecstasy Attacked—
Ecstasy Defended*

A Dastardly Attack on Ecstasy

In the September 1963 issue of *Esquire,* an article entitled "Getting Alienated with the Right Crowd at Harvard" carried a vigorous attack on ex-Harvard teachers Dr. Richard Alpert and Dr. Timothy Leary and the International Federation for Internal Freedom (IFIF). The author, Martin Mayer, leveled the following charges:

1. Leary and Alpert are like . . . ."laxative salesmen"
2. Leary and Alpert are . . . ."promoting drug consumption"
3. Leary and Alpert have formed . . . ."a drug cult"
4. Leary and Alpert promote . . . ."the symptoms of psychosis'"
5. Leary and Alpert promote . . . ."pathologies"
6. Leary and Alpert promote . . . ."brain damage by accident"
7. Leary and Alpert promote . . . ."brains damaged by the surgeon's knife"
8. Leary and Alpert are . . . ."promoting drug consumption"

* An abridged version of this chapter was published in *Esquire,* November 1963. Ralph Metzner and Richard Alpert helped with it.

9. Leary and Alpert are forming a......"drug cult"

10. Leary and Alpert are fostering........"pathologies"

11. Leary and Alpert are promoting a...."drug-induced psychosis"

12. Leary and Alpert are claiming the...."universal   failure of psychologists"

13. Leary and Alpert are having........"a whale of a time"

14. Leary and Alpert are causing........ "a terrifyingly bad time"

15. Leary and Alpert's experiments are...."utterly   valueless"

16. Leary and Alpert are..............."experimenters . . . who . . . got hooked on drugs"

17. Leary and Alpert are promoting......"hallucination"

18. Leary and Alpert are promoting a...."deathlike state"

19. Leary and Alpert were............."AWOL from classes"

20. Leary and Alpert are encouraging...."popular   misconceptions about marijuana"

21. Leary and Alpert are the..........."despair of . . . their . . . neighbors"

22. Leary and Alpert's.................."neighbors . . . have . . . gone to court to get rid of them"

23. Leary and Alpert adopt an.........."apparent intellectual respectability"

24. Leary and Alpert live in a..........."spiritual   Disneyland"

25. Leary and Alpert opened............."a psilocybin dram bin"

26. Leary and Alpert will get the......."boom lowered on them"

27. Leary and Alpert are like...........“fanatic Communists”

28. Leary and Alpert are like...........“overexuberant Catholic converts”

29. Leary and Alpert advocate the........“unrestrained civilian use of drugs”

30. Leary and Alpert are...............“very casual”

31. Leary and Alpert suffer from........“delusions of grandeur”

32. Leary and Alpert gave their..........“reluctant pledge not to use under-graduates”

33. Leary and Alpert are...............“socially with-drawn”

34. Leary and Alpert are...............“insensitive”

35. Leary and Alpert are...............“impulsive”

36. Leary and Alpert have an...........“unrealistic sense of omniscience”

37. Leary and Alpert are...............“psychosis peddling”

38. Leary and Alpert are...............“immoral”

39. Leary and Alpert...................“seem likely to wind up in places where they can be closely observed”

40. Leary and Alpert...................“can turn them-selves on at will”

41. Leary and Alpert deny that..........“psilocybin may do semipermanent physiological damage”

42. Leary and Alpert fail to realize that LSD “may be more dangerous than the more obviously addicting drugs”

43. Leary and Alpert argue.............."that man can become truly free
only by handing
over his cortex to a
drug company"

44. Leary and Alpert are..............."promoting mind-
distorting drugs"

45. Leary and Alpert encourage people to
play..............................."Russian roulette"

46. Leary and Alpert demonstrate that...."if you take drugs,
you are in no
condition to judge
them"

47. Leary and Alpert act like..........."holy rollers"

48. Leary and Alpert have become......."extremely
irrational"

49. Leary and Alpert have become......."conspiratorial"

50. Leary and Alpert..................."deny relevance to
all who do not
share the faith"

51. Leary and Alpert insist that non-drug
takers ...."are damned"

52. Leary and Alpert have developed a...."capacity for
concealment"

53. Leary and Alpert are..............."rivals for title of
world's worst
bores"

54. Leary and Alpert are..............."astonishingly
flamboyant"

55. Leary and Alpert..................."destroyed their
cause"

56. Leary and Alpert..................."will end up like
group (s) who had
police clubs
bounced off their
heads to chase
them out"

This multicount indictment was apparently based on an interview with Professor David McClelland, chairman of Harvard's department of social relations. Professor McClelland is a sincere, honorable man not ordinarily given to slandering and abusing his friends and his intellectual rivals in the popular press. The customary outlets for scientific and scholarly differences of opinion are professional journals, whose rules of evidence and reliance on empirical data are generally adhered to. Professor McClelland has indicated that he regrets this interview and the malicious twist it was given by Martin Mayer.

Cause for Alarm?

Mr. Martin Mayer is alarmed. Maybe he should be. These are scary times. The dangers and potentials of man's increasing ability to release and use external energy, electronic-atomic, are familiar to us all. But the fact that we now possess (in the drugs LSD, psilocybin and mescaline) simple and sure means of drastically altering man's *internal* situation, of releasing powerful neurological energy, is even more awesome.

Blow the Eight Million Minds of New York City

And changing man's consciousness is exactly what can now be done. The only aspect of the LSD controversy about which all parties do agree is that the new consciousness-expanding drugs are powerful. A standard "dose" of LSD is one hundred millionths of a gram. One pound of LSD could therefore blow the minds of the entire population of New York City.

Because of the importance of the issue, it is certainly valuable to have critical appraisals of what scientists are doing with these extraordinary mind-changing chemicals. Martin Mayer's article, if nothing else, is useful testimony that partisanship on these matters can become "furious" and "irrational" and "flamboyant," to use three of his favorite epithets. But such an extreme presentation as Mr. Mayer's should be in the form of a dialogue. It would be unfortunate if *Esquire* readers were not acquainted with the evidence and the opinions of that sizable group of scientists, scholars, religious leaders who have been led to different conclusions.

Who Are We?

Rather than litigate the more than 50 libelous and defamatory implications of the McClelland-Mayer story one by one, we prefer to present a list of statistics and quotations from published scientific documents which may explain why we happily left Harvard and why over 200 scientists and scholars are risking professional ostracism in order to continue research on the nonpsychiatric implications of consciousness-expanding foods and drugs.

We Are Industrious and Very Respectable

First of all, what is IFIF? IFIF is the independent research foundation started when Alpert and I left Harvard in 1963. The group who selected this wry double conditional for their title is composed of over 1,000 respectable Americans, mostly psychologists, ministers, academics, creative artists who want to conduct research in the potentialities of their own nervous systems by means of psychedelic foods and drugs. There are more than 200 doctors of psychology and medicine among the members. Mr. Mayer suggests that our group is in danger of "winding up in places where they will be closely observed." He need not worry. The first board of directors of IFIF consisted of 5 Harvard psychologists, a Harvard psychopharmacologist, 3 doctors of philosophy with additional theological degrees, and a professor at a well-known theological seminary. The scientific and scholarly output of this group is well recognized in the academic community. They have published dozens of books and well over a hundred articles in psychological and philosophical journals. Of the original IFIF board 6 have received Harvard doctorates, 2 have doctorates from Berkeley, 1 from Stanford, and the 10th, a doctorate of divinity.

What Have We Been Doing?

The stated purpose of IFIF was "to encourage support and protect research on psychedelic substances . . . and to take responsibility for serious studies in this area." To implement these goals, IFIF formed a number of research groups and projects all over the country which were ready to embark on systematic studies of consciousness expansion (until the federal government banned the drug). We started and have maintained for four years the only scholarly-scientific journal in the field—the *Psychedelic Review*. Experimental transcendental communities were established in Mexico, in Massachusetts and in Millbrook, New York, to apply psychedelic experiences to new forms of social living. New methods for recording and charting experiences of altered consciousness have been developed.

We have used every form of communication to turn on the American people to the love-joy within. We have made movies, cut records, chattered and chanted on TV, rapped on the radio, preached, done vaudeville routines, published prayer books, manuals, scientific articles. We have taught those who would listen what we have learned about ecstatic methods—incense, candles, flowers, bells, beads, yoga, meditation, Sufi dancing, shrines in the home, kinetic multichannel art, Hesse, Tolkein, Bosch, acid-rock, Hinduism, mantras, mudras, Tantra, psychedelic mating, leaving the city, avoiding plastic, walking barefoot and laughing-eyed, chanting love-seed delight.

While several million Americans listened to our message, the people who run the spaceship have cried with one swelling metal voice—ecstasy is bad, ecstasy is escape, ecstasy is dangerous!

Why?

The Ancient Struggle of the Metal Men against the Flower People

History may provide one answer. R. Gordon Wasson, a retired vice-president of Morgan Guaranty Trust and himself a Harvard research fellow, has marshaled considerable evidence indicating that the persecution of mind-expanding foods and drugs is not new but indeed began when the first Europeans came to the New World. Three hallucinogenic plants were used by the Indians of Mexico before the conquest: peyote, the sacred mushroom, and ololiuqui. Mr. Wasson refers to "the importance . . . attributed to these plants, and the strangely moving episodes that . . . tell of the Indians' utter faith and defense of them. . . . The civilization of Europe had known nothing like these novel drugs of Mexico, at least not in recorded history. Similar miraculous powers were attributed in a way to the elements in the mass; and the Catholic Church . . . was quick to perceive this, to it, alarming parallel. But belief in the divinity of the Sacrament called for an act of faith, whereas the Mexican plants spoke for themselves. In a number of situations the record is clear: the friars conceded the miracle wrought by these agents but attributed them to the machinations of the Evil One." Fear and smear of psychedelic drugs is far from new.

In speaking of the hallucinogenic morning glory seeds known as ololiuqui, Wasson says, "Throughout these references of the Spanish historians there runs a note of somber poignancy as we see two cultures in a duel to the death,—on the one hand, the fanaticism of sincere Churchmen, hotly pursuing with the support of the harsh secular arm what they considered a superstition and an idolatry; on the other, the tenacity and wile of the Indians defending their cherished ololiuqui."

The active ingredients of the three plants which Wasson describes in these passages have now been synthesized by chemists and called mescaline (peyote), psilocybin (the sacred mushroom), and LSD (ololiuqui). It is these three drugs which have stirred up the current verbal and legal debate.

Prohibition Is Superstitious

Now listen to the modern voice of Alan Watts, distinguished philosopher and onetime Harvard research associate, speaking of the same three drugs: "The grounds for any possible suppression of these medicines are almost entirely superstitious. There

is no evidence for their being as deleterious as alcohol or tobacco, nor, indeed, for their being harmful in any way except
when used in improper circumstances, or perhaps with psychotic subjects. They are considerably less dangerous than many
of the ordinary contents of the family medicine cupboard or
kitchen closet. As instruments of power and inquiry they do not
even begin to be as risky as X rays, and as threats to mental
health they can hardly match the daily drivel assailing our
thoughts through radio, television, and the newspaper."

*No critic of LSD—journalistic or psychiatric—has yet cited a
convincing statistic or made reference to a published scientific
study demonstrating danger,* and yet the hysteria over these
drugs mounts and the "harsh secular arm" of the government
and the medical associations cracks down.* The *Medical Tribune,* in an editorial on March 18, 1963, reported that these
drugs "have been demonstrated to be physically safe," and then
on June 17, 1963, reliable sources told the *Medical Tribune*
that "district branches of the American Psychiatric Association
are seriously contemplating disciplinary action against certain
of their members who had developed large 'LSD practices.' "

The Trip Can Take You Anywhere

One reason for the struggle over the interpretation and use of
these drugs is the wide variation in their effect. Chemicals like
LSD cause no specific response beyond their general tendency
to speed up and drastically expand awareness. The specific effect
is almost entirely due to the preparations for the session and the
surroundings—the set and the setting. In this respect, the person's reaction to his initial LSD session is much like his first
reaction to his first sexual experience. If he is psychologically
prepared and if the setting is voluntary and pleasant, then a
whole new world of experience opens up. But if the initial

---

* These lines were written on July 1, 1968. The government has paid for,
promoted and widely publicized three or four anti-LSD experiments (sub-
sequently disproved) and then openly claimed credit for "scaring" young people
away from the sacrament. Deliberate hoax.

experience occurs with inadequate preparation or fearful expectation and if the experience is involuntary and the setting impersonal, then a most distasteful reaction is inevitable. Psychiatrists have regularly given LSD to research subjects in circumstances where they did not know what was going to happen (double-blind experimentation) and where the surroundings were bleak, clinical, public, and anxiety-provoking. Such a procedure, even in the guise of science, is nothing short of psychological rape, and it is exactly this sort of impersonal laboratory experimentation which has given LSD a bad name in medical circles.

So much for the so-called dangers. What of the benefits and applications? Dr. Sanford M. Unger, a government research psychologist, has written a review entitled "Mescaline, LSD, Psilocybin, and the Issue of Rapid Personality Change." Doctor Unger is witty, skeptical, but thorough. He has prepared an annotated bibliography of 52 psychiatric studies which document the curative powers of these drugs. Let us take a brief look at some of the areas in which LSD has been found to be of help.

1. *Alcoholics.* Several independent studies in Canada have found that 50 to 60 percent of alcoholics given one session with LSD stay "dry" for follow-up periods from 6 months to 1 year. In 1961 LSD treatment was designated as the officially recognized method for curing alcoholism in the province of Saskatchewan and was considered "no longer experimental."

2. *Neurotics.* Savage reports that of 96 patients who had undergone one intense, well-prepared LSD session, 85 percent claimed lasting benefit; 78 percent felt it was "the greatest thing that ever happened to me." The reported benefits included "ability to love, to handle hostility, to communicate, greater understanding, improved relations with others, decreased anxiety, increased self-esteem, increased effectiveness in work, and a new way of looking at the world. . . . The data would seem to indicate that the felt benefits tend to become apparent some time after the LSD experience and to be sustained fairly well over at least the first year following."

3. *Criminals.* Leary, in a study of convicts at a Massachusetts state prison, reports that inmates in the treatment program which used psilocybin increased in "responsibility" and "self-control" and decreased in "psychopathy" compared to a control group who had not received the drug. The psilocybin group also had a recidivism rate that was lower by 23 percent than the normally expected rate, which is over 50 percent.

4. *Disturbed Adolescents.* Kenneth Cameron has reported on the successful use of LSD with several disturbed adolescents with whom all other forms of treatment had failed.

5. *Childhood Schizophrenics.* Lauretta Bender, director of research and child psychiatry for the New York State Department of Mental Hygiene, has reported at a recent meeting that in three groups of autistic and schizophrenic children, LSD had produced "behavior changes without any of the acute psychotic symptoms observed in adults."

6. *Terminal Cancer Patients.* In a study with 50 advanced-cancer patients, Dr. Eric Kast of the Chicago Medical School has shown that small doses of LSD relieved pain for 32 hours, compared to the 2 or 3 hours' analgesia with traditional pain-killers. "The emotions invested in the sickness are temporarily diverted in otherworldly or 'transcendental' directions. The patients minimize the sense of impending disaster with an effect inappropriate to our Western civilization, but most beneficial to their own psychic states."

Thus there seems little doubt that LSD and other psychedelics have proven useful enough in a large variety of personal disturbances to at least warrant further unprejudiced research. Of course, the efficacy of LSD has not been established by the most rigorous scientific standards; but for that matter, neither has the efficacy of any other form of psychological treatment been so established. There has never been, in the history of medicine, a method applicable to so many conditions, from alcoholism to cancer, which is so rapid and effective in such minute doses.

What about the effects of LSD on "normal" people? In 4 separate studies by different investigators comprising more than 400 subjects, LSD and psilocybin produced experience of lasting benefit or change in 64 percent of the subjects and "a pleasant experience" in 73 percent of the subjects.* An average of 80 percent wanted to repeat the experience. Is it not strange that an experience which is regarded with such fear and distrust by those who have not had it is so highly regarded by those who have?

It Makes You Feel So Good

The evidence that LSD produces rapid, even sudden, cures for emotional disorders is threatening enough. Next comes the evidence that the process could be enjoyable, even ecstatic. That something which is "good for you" can also be pleasant is perhaps the most fearful pill of all for a puritan culture to swallow.

In a study by Savage, 85 percent reported "a very pleasant experience" and 81 percent "an experience of great beauty." Exactly two-thirds of Janiger's subjects claim "a very pleasant experience"; 70 percent of subjects in a study by Leary describe "wonderful, ecstatic or very pleasant" reactions.

"I cried for joy," says psychologist Wilson Van Deusen about his LSD session. "I will have enjoyed more living in the latter part of my life than most people ever know," says Cary Grant in summarizing his LSD results. "A possession by the spirit of wholeness," says philosopher Gerald Heard. "A repeated flow of beauty to heightened beauty from deeper to ever deeper meaning. Words like 'grace' and 'transfiguration' came to my mind," writes Aldous Huxley. "Extraordinary joy overcame me . . . a strong and beautiful feeling of eternity and infinity," chronicles Beringer, the famous Heidelberg neurologist. "A New Artificial Paradise," and "A Divine Plant" were the titles of papers by Havelock Ellis describing his mescal experiences.

Now such words as *joy, ecstasy, grace, beauty,* just don't exist in the psychiatric vocabulary. The poor psychiatrist has been given the sad task of looking for pathology. He's happiest when he's found problems and is usually bewildered when he comes

* *Psychedelic Review,* No. 1.

face-to-face with the more meaningful experiences of life. This dilemma is nicely illustrated in a wistful comment by a well-known psychiatrist in the 1955 round table on LSD and mescaline sponsored by the American Psychiatric Association: "I should like to confess that my experience with mescaline was an exceedingly pleasant one. I found myself in my enthusiasm using words like 'mystical' and 'ecstatic,' until I found my colleagues raising their eyebrows at this, and looking at me askance; after which I simply described it as 'very pleasant.'"

LSD Turns You On to God

That LSD produces ecstasy and sudden cure was probably reason enough for its being banned in America, but there was news ahead which increased the medical opposition. Evidence started turning up that psychedelic drugs produced religious experiences. Horrors! In the study by Savage, 90 percent of subjects claimed "a greater awareness of God or a higher power." Studies published by Leary revealed that over two-thirds of a sample of 67 ministers, monks, and rabbis reported the deepest spiritual experience of their lives. And in a double-blind, controlled study run on Good Friday, 1963, in the Boston University Chapel, 9 out of 10 divinity students shakingly recounted awesome mystical-religious experiences, and 2 of them promptly quit the ministry! "The drugs make an end run around Christ and go straight to the Holy Spirit," was the paradoxical comment of Theodore Gill, president of San Francisco's Presbyterian Theological Seminary. The words of William James, generally held to be the greatest psychologist America has ever produced, were remembered: "Looking back on my experiences [with nitrous oxide] they all converge toward an insight to which I cannot help ascribing some metaphysical significance."

According to *Time* magazine, "Clerics . . . charge that LSD zealots have become a clique of modern gnostics concerned only with furthering their private search for what they call 'inner freedom.' Others feel that the church should not quickly dismiss anything that has the power to deepen faith. Dr. W. T. Stace of Princeton, one of the nation's foremost students of mysticism, believes that LSD can change lives for the better. 'The fact that the experience was induced by drugs has no bearing on its validity,' he says."

Police Clubs Bouncing Off Our Heads

At this point we remember Mr. Wasson's poignant account of the religious struggle between the Indians (who called the Mexican mushroom "God's flesh") and the agents of the Spanish Inquisition. *Esquire*'s Martin Mayer may have been saying more than he wished to reveal when he compared IFIF to a group of heretical Catholic converts, to fundamentalist Protestants, and to Christian Scientists in a context insulting to all three religious groups. Mr. Mayer predicted that IFIF will end up like Catholic converts with "police clubs bouncing off their heads"; he may be telling us less about LSD than about the state of *his own* intolerance for any heretical deviation from *his* favored orthodoxies.

We Want to Have Fun and Be Good Scientists, Too

Professor McClelland and Mr. Mayer make a great point of saying that IFIF is no longer a scientific group. The term "science" has apparently become a sacred term forbidden to innovating theorists and methodologists. It is true that we have often dispensed with the rituals of modern psychology. This is not because of naïveté or carelessness but from a thoughtful reconsideration of the philosophy of behavior and consciousness. Again, the popular press is not the place to discuss scholarly differences. Interested readers can find our criticisms and constructive alternatives in the scientific literature, consisting of new methods, forms, instruments and hypotheses designed and used by IFIF experimenters.

The accusation is also made that IFIF is anti-intellectual. It is true that we are most dissatisfied with the intellectual narrowness and naïveté of much of modern psychology and that we have taken as our central task the production of more effective and sophisticated concepts. We are indeed trying most energetically to outmode current theories of human nature as fast as we can. We do not see this as either rebellion or heresy but rather as the traditional goal of the intellectual-scientific game. We also believe that all human activities, including the scientific, are funny.

Have You or Haven't You? That Is the Question

The debate over psychedelic drugs invariably breaks down into two groups: those that have had the experience versus those that have not. As R. Gordon Wasson has pointed out with gentle sarcasm, "We are all divided into two classes: those who have taken the mushroom and are disqualified by the subjective experience, and those who have not taken the mushroom and are disqualified by their total ignorance of the subject." Or as comedian Dave Gardner puts it, "How are you gonna explain anything to anyone who hasn't ever?"

But we seem to need more than the inexperience-experience difference or our American puritanical heritage to explain why the "moral, religious, social" applications of psychedelic drugs can be experienced so freely and humorously in other countries and why such research is shut down in America with the undocumented cries of "morbidity," "mortality," "danger," "immoral."

Get Your Sterile, Surgical Rubber Gloves Off My Soul, Doctor Farnsworth

The political role of medicine and psychiatry may have something to do with this difference. In other countries, physicians and psychiatrists are respected and well-paid members of the professional class. That and nothing more. In the United States these disciplines aspire to and lobby for a position of political and moral monopoly which is beyond criticism or debate. Dr. Dana Farnsworth, our psychiatric rival at Harvard, in his anti-

LSD editorial in the *Journal of the American Medical Association* is bold enough to make this astounding statement: "The ingestion or injection or inhalation of any agent taken or given to alter a person's usual mental and emotional equilibrium must be looked upon as a medical procedure. These agents should, therefore, be under medical control. . . ." Snuff out your cigarette, boy, and forget your before-dinner martini, and throw out your wife's perfume bottle. Ladies and gentlemen, you've just lost a freedom you never realized you had to protect —the right to taste, smell, breathe or otherwise introduce into your own body anything which will change your mind or your mood. When we talk about "internal freedom" and "the politics of the nervous system," we are foreseeing and forewarning about invasions of personal liberty which no longer date to the brave new world of 1984. Our debate with psychiatrists about the use and control of psychedelic drugs involves the right, right now, of thoughtful Americans to change their own consciousness.

Training for Ecstasy

A final clarification. Mr. Mayer and others have accused us of advocating indiscriminate availability and use of consciousness-expanding drugs. The facts are exactly to the contrary. IFIF has been more outspoken than any other group in the country in advocating the need for experience and training in the use of these extraordinarily powerful tools. The experience, however, must come from the drug itself, and the training must be specialized. No present medical or psychological degree qualifies for the job. A medical degree doesn't equip one to pilot a jet plane or to understand the incredible complexities of consciousness. The LSD experience is so novel and so powerful that the more you think you know about the mind, the more astounded and even frightened you'll be when your consciousness starts to flip you out of your mind. A new profession of psychedelic guides will inevitably develop to supervise these experiences. The training for this new profession will aim at producing the patience of a first-grade teacher, the humility and wisdom of a Hindu guru, the loving dedication of a minister-priest, the sensitivity of a poet, and the imagination of a science fiction writer.

Do You or Don't You?

The debate could and inevitably will be continued—in the press, in the scholarly journals, in conversations and within people's minds. Sooner or later everyone will have to answer for himself the simple basic question, do you or don't you? Do you want to turn on or don't you? Do you want to expand your awareness or not? Transcendence—becoming aware of a reality which lies outside of time, space and the beloved ego—has been a basic privilege and goal of man since earliest times. In our present age, writes Carl G. Jung in his autobiography, "man has been robbed of transcendence by the shortsightedness of the super-intellectual." A large number of serious and responsible citizens, along with a million or so young people, believe and have stated that transcendence can be brought about by the psychedelic chemicals, given suitable preparation and an appropriate setting.

But such a view has too many far-reaching consequences to be accepted on the basis of verbal debate. Each man must experience it for himself.

This article is unlikely to convince anyone or change anyone's opinion. If it will make some readers of *Esquire* aware that a different view is possible than the one expressed in Mr. Mayer's article, our purpose will have been accomplished. Let us recall to mind the words Hermann Hesse, the Nobel Prize novelist and philosopher, wrote in *Siddhartha:*

> Words do not express thoughts very well; everything immediately becomes a little different, a little distorted, a little foolish. And yet it is also pleasing and seems right that what is of value and wisdom to one man seems nonsense to another.

Peace, Mr. Martin Mayer.

5

Chemical Warfare—The Alcoholics
vs. the Psychedelics

Marijuana alters consciousness.

LSD alters consciousness.

On that they all agree.

Policeman. Priest. Pusher. Politician. Prophet. Pharmacologist. Psychologist. Policeman.

They all agree that marijuana and LSD turn us on.

But how?

And to what end—evil or beneficial?

To these questions there is no agreement.

Sincere, well-intentioned men are led to extreme positions. On the one hand—punitive laws, repressive crusades, police action, the arming of agents of Health, Education and Welfare, the lengthy imprisonment of citizens for no other crime than the altering of their own consciousness.

According to *Life* magazine, "One of the stiffest and most inflexible set of laws ever put to the federal books, the Boggs-Daniel Act (1956) represents the high-water mark of punitive legislation against the use, sale and handling of drugs. It imposed severe mandatory sentences for sale or possession—permitting in most cases neither probation nor parole. . . .

"In some states, such as New York, sentencing is fairly lenient. Mere possession (25 or more marijuana cigarettes . . .) carries sentence of only (*sic*) three to ten years."

San Francisco magazine reports, "In today's affluent society

[87

the use of marijuana is no longer confined to the 'dregs' of society. It is becoming increasingly fashionable with middle and upper-class youth. California jails now hold close to 6,000 people for breaking marijuana laws. Sixty-four percent of all Californians arrested on marijuana charges are under twenty-five years of age. Arrests for breaking marijuana laws . . . since 1962 . . . have increased nearly 500 percent."

On the other hand—passive resistance, poetic and artistic and scientific appeals to reason, futile protests, flights into exile, cynicism.

"Dr. S. J. Holmes, director of the narcotics addiction unit of the Alcoholism and Drug Addiction Research Foundation in Toronto . . . believes it is 'fantastic and ridiculous' that a person caught with one marijuana cigarette can be sent to prison.

"It is particularly ridiculous, he said, when compared with the use and effect of alcohol. 'This situation is really a disgrace to our civilization and merits much consideration.'

"The preliminary estimates of a foundation-financed study on drug use at San Francisco State show that 60 percent of the students will at some time use an illegal drug. . . .

"Marijuana is sold on the campus, smoked on the campus, and used by professors.

"A Berkeley sorority girl said, 'When you drink you lose control and sensitivity, generally feeling and acting like a slobbering idiot. This never happens with pot.

"Most spoke of the legal problems, as did this girl: 'It doesn't bother me to break the law. How many times do you break it jaywalking and so on? The main thing is that I just don't think of using marijuana in these terms. It's pure hypocrisy and stupidity that it's not legal. The law is wrong for both practical and moral reasons."

Cheetah magazine, December 1967, reports that one outlaw LSD manufacturer alone had released 10 million doses.

A UPI wire story from Washington, December 28, 1967, presents an interesting sidelight on "how we won the war in Vietnam."

"John Steinbeck IV, son of the Nobel Prize-winning author, said Wednesday that 75 percent of U.S. soldiers in Vietnam smoke marijuana. But the Defense Department said the figure was 'beyond all reason.'

"Steinbeck, twenty-one, who spent a year in Vietnam with the Army, said use of the drug did not seriously affect a soldier's fighting ability, but made the horrors of combat easier to endure.

"The Army is investigating marijuana use in Vietnam but has not commented on the results of its study, although it has been reported that the Army found that 83 percent of its troops use the drug."

There are many dimensions to the psychedelic drug controversy and no simple answers. I wish to consider in this essay three issues—the political, the moral, and the scientific.

Who Is Fighting Whom and Why?

To understand the psychedelic controversy, it is necessary to study the sociology of psychedelic drugs. Who wants to get high? Who wants to smoke marijuana? To eat peyote? To ingest LSD? What people comprise this new drug menace?

The young

The racially and nationally alienated

The creative

Over 90 percent of the users of psychedelic plants and drugs fall into at least one of these three categories.

The Young Want to Turn On

Over 50 percent of the American population is under the age of twenty-five. Ominous, isn't it? From 50 to 70 percent of the usage of marijuana and LSD is by the high school and college age group. Around 70 percent of the arrests and imprisonments for possession of psychedelic substances fall on the shoulders of those under the age of thirty. The whiskey-drinking menopausal imprison the pot-smoking youth. Meditate on this situation.

The Racially and Nationally Alienated Like to Turn On

Negroes, Puerto Ricans, American Indians. The usage of the psychedelic plants marijuana and peyote in these noble minority groups of the American society is high. The whiskey-drinking, white middle class imprisons those with different cultural and religious preferences. Meditate on this situation.

The Creative Have to Turn On

It is conservative to estimate that over 70 percent of non-academic creative artists have used psychedelic substances in their work.

Painters. Poets. Musicians. Dancers. Actors. Directors. Beatle-brows. The whiskey-drinking middlebrows imprison the growing edge. Meditate on this situation.

The Criminal and Psychedelic Drugs

The stereotyped picture of the marijuana smoker is that of a criminal type. The statistics do not support this myth. Marijuana is used by groups which are socially alienated from middle-aged values—youth, Negroes, Indians, creative artists—but few criminals. Alcohol is the drug of the middle-aged white criminal. The larcenous and the violent. Safecrackers and Marines. The economics of heroin leads the addict to steal. Few professional criminals smoke pot. Few pot smokers are criminals (except for the offense of changing their consciousness) .

The Psychedelic Majority Group

The number of pot smokers worldwide is larger than the population of the United States of America! It is safe to say that there are more pot smokers than there are members of the middle class throughout the world! Indeed, we have the astonishing spectacle of a small, menopausal, middle-class minority, tolerant to alcohol and addicted to external power, passing laws against and interfering with the social-religious rituals of a sizable and growing majority! Meditate on that one.

In this country the number of persons who have used marijuana, peyote, and LSD is estimated to be over 20 million. Remember the Indians, Negroes, the young, the creative. We deal here with one of the largest persecuted groups in the country. Until recently this sizable group has been nonvocal. Effectively prevented from presenting its case. Essentially stripped of its constitutional rights.

Another crucial sociological issue which is easily overlooked—psychedelic people tend to be socially passive. The psychedelic experience is by nature private, sensual, spiritual, internal, introspective. Whereas alcohol and amphetamines stimulate the efferent nervous system, inciting furious game activities, the psychedelics stimulate the afferent nervous centers. Contemplation. Meditation. Sensual openness. Artistic and religious preoccupation.

Excesses of passive contemplation are little better than excesses of action—but certainly no worse. God and the DNA code designed men to have interoceptive and exteroceptive neurological systems, and any harmonious view of man should allow for judicious and thoughtful balancing of both.

Throughout world history the psychedelic people have not tended to form commissions to stamp out nonpsychedelic people. Nor do they pass laws against or imprison nonpsychedelicists. Pot smokers don't throw whiskey drinkers in jail.

The Molecular Revolution

Politically oriented activists have throughout history left the psychedelic minority pretty much alone. The power holders have been too busy fighting each other to worry about those who prefer to live in quiet harmony and creative quietude.

It is harder work to contact and control your nervous system than the external symbol structure. Yogis, bhikkus, meditators, Sufis, monks, shamen, hashish mystics have been too busy decoding and appreciating their afferent (sensory) and cellular communication systems to busy themselves with political struggles.

But now comes the molecular revolution. The work of James McConnell demonstrates that learning is molecular. Dumb flatworms eat smart flatworms and become smart. Holger Hyden discovers that the brain cells of educated rats contain a third more RNA than those of uneducated rats. University of California psychologists pass on learning from one rat to another by injecting RNA from trained rats.

Neurologists are "wiring up" the brains of animals and men and altering consciousness by pressing buttons. Press a button—make him hungry. Press a button—make him horny. Press a button—make him angry. Press a button—make him happy.

The psychedelic chemicals flood out of the laboratories. Into the hands of the two familiar groups: those who want to do something to others for power and control; those who want to do something to themselves for fun and love.

U.S. Army psychologists secretly drop LSD into the coffee of an infantry platoon. The surprised soldiers giggle, break ranks and wander off, looking at the trees. Psychiatrists secretly drop LSD into the water glasses of psychotic patients and report that LSD enhances insanity!

And on the college campuses and in the art centers of the country, hundreds of thousands of the creative young take LSD and millions smoke marijuana to explore their own consciousness. The new cult of visionaries. They turn on, tune in, and often drop out.

Laws are passed encouraging the administration of LSD to the unsuspecting (patients, soldiers, research subjects) and preventing self-administration!

The Two Commandments of the Molecular Age

Of the many powerful energies now suddenly available to man, the most challenging and sobering are those which alter the fabric of thought and judgment—the very core of meaning and being.

Learning, memory, mood, judgment, identity, consciousness can now, today, be instantaneously transformed by electrical and chemical stimuli.

In the long-short diary of our species, no issue has passed such a promise-peril.

The history of human evolution (not unlike that of every other species of life on our planet) is the record of new forms of energy—physical, mechanical, chemical—discovered, slowly understood and misunderstood, painfully debated, eventually adapted to.

Today the human race is confronted with new energies which tax our wisdom, confuse our judgment, terrorize our emotional securities, excite our highest aspirations and threaten to alter our central notions of man and his place on this planet.

Never has man faced ethical and political issues so complex, so delicate, so demanding, so frightening.

Never has man been in greater need of ethical guidance.

And where is it?

Our scientists plunge enthusiastically into the process of consciousness alteration, with little apparent regard for the moral and political complications.

One of the few men who have recognized the high stakes of this new game of cerebral roulette is David Krech, psychologist at Berkeley.

Doctor Krech is quoted as saying: "Until recently, these substances were considered science fiction, but real science has been moving forward so rapidly in this area that science fiction is hard put to keep up with it. About fifteen years ago, I doubt whether I could have found more than a half dozen laboratories in the entire world which were concerned with basic research in behavior, brain and biochemistry. Today there hardly exists a major laboratory where such research is not being given high priority.

"If we should find effective mind-control agents," he says, "we must consider whether the manufacture and dispensing of such agents should be left to private enterprise, or to military control, or to political control. And how should this be done, and when, and by whom? It is not too early for us to ponder very seriously the awesome implications of what brain research may discover."

The time has come for a new ethical code to deal with issues unforeseen (or were they, really?) by our earlier prophets and moralists.

Although the social-political implications are hopelessly complicated, the moral issues are clear-cut, precisely pure. And if the moral center of gravity is maintained, the endless chain of political and administrative decisions can be dealt with confidently and serenely.

Two new ethical commandments are necessary as man moves into the molecular age. Compared to these imperatives, the codes of earlier prophets seem like game rules—codes for social harmony. The new commandments are neurological and biochemical in essence—and therefore, I suspect, in closer harmony with the laws of cellular wisdom, the law of the DNA code.

I did not invent these commandments. They are the result of several hundred psychedelic sessions. They are revealed to me by my nervous system, by ancient cellular counsel. I give them to you as revelation. I ask you not to take them on faith but to check them out with your own nervous system. I urge you to memorize these two commandments. Meditate on them. Pin the next page to your wall. I urge you to take 300 gamma of LSD and present these commandments to your symbol-free nervous system. The future of our species depends upon your understanding of and obedience to these two natural laws. Ask your nervous system. Ask your DNA code.

THE TWO COMMANDMENTS
FOR THE MOLECULAR AGE

I Thou shalt not alter the consciousness
of thy fellow man.

II Thou shalt not prevent thy fellow man
from altering his own consciousness.

Commentary on the Two Commandments

Thousands of theological, philosophical and legal texts will be written in the next few decades interpreting, qualifying, specifying these two commandments. I happily leave this chore to those who face the implementation of this code. But a few general comments may be helpful.

1. These commandments are not new. They are specifications of the first Mosaic law—that man shall not act as God to others. Be God yourself, if you can, but do not impose your divinity on others. They are also specifications of the two Christian commandments—thou shalt love God and thy fellow man.

2. There are several obvious qualifications of the first commandment. Do not alter the consciousness of your fellow man by symbolic, electrical, chemical, molecular means. If he wants you to? Yes. You can help him alter his own consciousness. Or you can get his conscious, alerted permission to alter his consciousness—for him in the direction he wants, etc.

3. There are several obvious qualifications of the second commandment. The First Amendment constrains us from preventing our fellow man from altering his consciousness by means of symbols. This is the familiar "freedom of expression" issue. But now we must not prevent our fellow man from altering his own consciousness by chemical, electrical or molecular means. These are new freedoms which the wise men who wrote the American Constitution and the Rights of Man did not anticipate, but which they certainly would have included if they had known.

4. Can you prevent your fellow man from altering his consciousness if he thereby poses a threat to others or to the harmonious development of society? Yes. But be careful. You walk near a precarious precipice. Whenever society restricts the freedom of the human being to alter his own consciousness (by means of symbols or chemicals), the burden of proof as to danger to others must be on society. We can prevent others

from doing things which restrict our consciousness—but the justification must be clear.

The Scientific Approach to Psychedelic Chemicals

The political and ethical controversies over psychedelic plants are caused by our basic ignorance about what these substances do.

They alter consciousness.

But how, where, why, what for?

Questions about psychedelic drugs remain unanswered because our basic questions about consciousness remain unanswered.

As we learn more about the biochemistry and physiology of consciousness, then we will understand the specific effects and uses of consciousness-altering plants.

But external, look-at-it-from-the-outside science is not enough. Biochemistry and neurology will soon unravel some of the riddles of molecular learning and RNA[1] education. Blessings on James McConnell and David Krech and Holger Hyden. But then what? Who shall use the new magic molecules? Who shall control them? The routine scientoid solutions are: "Inject them in the stupid, inject them in the crazy, inject them into Army privates, inject them in the senile—and eventually, when they are safe enough to prevent lawsuits, sell them to the docile middle class."

But wait a minute, dear scientoids. We can't do that anymore. Remember? We are not dealing with molecules that blow up the enemy or eradicate insects or cure headaches or produce the mild stupor of alcohol or tranquilize the active. We are dealing

---

1 Within the nucleus of every living cell lies a tiny, complex chain of protein molecules called the DNA code. DNA is the brain of the cell, the timeless blueprinting code which designs every aspect of life. DNA executes its plans by means of RNA molecules. RNA is the communication system, the language, the senses and hands of the DNA. The language of RNA can be passed from one organism to another. The discovery of this fact is revolutionizing our theories of memory, learning, consciousness, and education. The basic unit of learning is molecular. The basic unit of consciousness is molecular.

with agents that change consciousness. And we have a new commandment to obey. Remember? "Thou shalt not alter the consciousness of thy fellow man."

And if society attempts to control the new molecules, then we have the black market problem all over again. You remember the LSD situation? The scientoid plan was to research LSD quietly in mental hospitals and Army bases, double-blindly drugging the unsuspecting. But the word got out—"LSD produces ecstasy. LSD helps you see through the game veil." And the revolution began. The upper-middle-class underground. The white collar black market.

And then the laws and the penalties and the arming of agents of the Department of Health, Education and Welfare to hunt down the psychedelic people.

> Any officer or employee of the department . . . may—
> 1. carry firearms
> 2. execute and serve search warrants
> 3. execute seizure
> 4. make arrests without warrants
>   (Drug Abuse Control Amendments of 1965)

And next come the "smart pills." Will the same cycle of dreary platitudes and bureaucratic hysteria take place again?

WASHINGTON, D.C. JANUARY 1, 1969. HEALTH, EDUCATION AND WELFARE OFFICIALS ANNOUNCE TODAY REGULATIONS CONTROLLING ILLICIT USE OF INTELLIGENCE-CREATIVITY PILLS.

ACCORDING TO THE NEW LAWS, DNA AND RNA MOLECULES CAN BE ADMINISTERED ONLY BY GOVERNMENT-APPROVED PHYSICIANS IN A GOVERNMENT-SUPPORTED HOSPITAL.

HARVARD BLACK MARKET BARED IN RNA.

SMART-PILL FAD NEW CAMPUS KICK.

Hey!

"Did you hear? There's a new shipment of black market Einstein, A. A., in the Village!"

"I'm giving my wife some Elizabeth Taylor nucleic acid for

Christmas. Smuggled in from Mexico. We can all afford to learn new methods, right?"

"I know it's against the law, but Willy is five years old and can't work quantum-theory equations. So, in despair, I've connected with some Max Planck RNA."

NEW YORK, APRIL 1, 1969, A.P.:

The newly organized microbiological unit of the Health, Education and Welfare Department, armed with paralysis spray guns and electron microscopes, raided an RNA den last night. Over one hundred million grams of amino acid were seized. Agents estimated that the haul was worth close to $800,000. Held on charges of being present on premises where illegal drugs were seized were a poet, a philosopher, and two college-age girls. HEW agents tentatively labeled the contraband molecules as Shakespeare RNA, Socrates RNA and Helen of Troy RNA.

R. Wilheim Phlymption, president of the American Psychiatric Association, Amino Acid Division, when notified of the raid, said: "Amino acids RNA and DNA are dangerous substances causing illegitimacy, suicide and irresponsible sexuality. They should be administered only by psychiatrists in government hospitals or Army research stations."

The four alleged drug cultists who were held on $25,000 bail smiled enigmatically but made no comment.

These headlines won't happen, will they? They can't happen, because now we have the two commandments for the molecular age.

The scientist must be prevented from experimenting on the brains of other people.

"Thou shalt not alter the consciousness of thy fellow man."

Congressmen, policemen, judges, and secret agents of the Department of Health, Education and Welfare must lay down their arms. Remember the second commandment:

"Thou shalt not prevent thy fellow man from altering his own consciousness."

Now that chemists have produced psychedelic chemicals and biochemists are isolating the powers of RNA, it comes time to face the real scientific issue.

The Scientist Must Take the Drug Himself

Consciousness and alteration of consciousness cannot be studied from the standpoint of external science, from the standpoint of look-at-it-from-the-outside science.

Not only does this violate the first commandment, it just doesn't work.

The meaning and use of psychedelic chemicals—LSD, STP, MDA, PCP, smart pills, RNA—depends on the scientist's taking the molecules himself, opening up his own consciousness, altering his own nervous system. Only in this way will we develop the maps, models, languages, techniques for utilizing the new mind-changing procedures.

You can't use these internal microscopes by clapping them over the eyes of unsuspecting mental patients and Army privates. The scientist has to look through them.

The mind-altering chemicals—lysergic acid, amino acids—have to be studied from within. The scientist has to take the love pill and the smart pill.

Oh, yes, you can observe their effects from outside, but this tells you very little. You can "sacrifice" the animals and discover brain changes. You can drug mental defectives and psychotics and seniles and terminal patients and observe gross behavior changes, but these are the irrelevant husks. Consciousness must be studied from within. Each psychedelic chemical opens a complex energy language which must be deciphered with exacting discipline and code-breaking ingenuity.

The molecular psychologist must decipher these languages. Eventually everyone will learn them. This is not a new idea. This is the core idea of all Eastern psychology. Buddhism, for example, is not a religion. It is a complex system of psychology, a series of languages and methods for decoding levels of consciousness.

And this is the original method of Western scientific psychology—the trained introspection of Wundt, Weber, Fechner, Titchener. The scientist must learn the language of the sensory neuron and cell and teach it to others.

The typical scientist recoils from this suggestion. It's a tough assignment, isn't it? No more dosing up the passive subjects. *You,* the scientist, must inhale, swallow, inject the magic molecule *yourself.* You train others to do the same.

The Courage to Know

Frightening?

Yes, it is frightening. And this defines the first criterion of the scientist of consciousness. He must have courage. He must embark on a course of planfully and deliberately going out of his mind. This is no field for the faint of heart. You are venturing out (like the Portuguese sailors, like the astronauts) on the uncharted margins. But be reassured—it's an old human custom. It's an old living-organism custom. We're here today because certain adventurous proteins, certain far-out experimenting cells, certain hippy amphibia, certain brave men pushed out and exposed themselves to new forms of energy.

Where do you get this courage?

It isn't taught in graduate school or medical school or law school. It doesn't come by arming government agents.

It comes from faith.

Faith in your nervous system.

Faith in your body.

Faith in your cells.

Faith in the life process.

Faith in the molecular energies released by psychedelic molecules.

Not blind faith.

Not faith in human social forms.

But conscious faith in the harmony and wisdom of nature.

Faith easily checked out empirically.

Take LSD and see. Listen to what your nervous system and your cells tell you.

Take marijuana and learn what your sense organs can tell you.

Take RNA and learn how the molecular learning process works.

Trust your body and its reaction to the complex messages of the psychedelic drugs.

SEAL OF THE LEAGUE

6

The Magical Mystery Trip

For the last few years, America has been on a Magical Mystery Trip, planned and guided by Englishmen.

THEY'VE BEEN GOING IN AND OUT OF FASH, BUT THEY'RE GUARANTEED TO BE A SMASH.

Everything harmonious and graceful in the electronic psychedelic revolution of the 1960's has come from the venerable East-Anglia Import-Export Company. The eye-land empire.

The English have seed style. The polished performance based on the rich racial myth. A hip DNA root structure that enables them instinctively to deal with the pulsing energies of our time—electronics and psychedelics.

ELEMENTARY PUT-ON SINGING MAHARISHI MAN YOU SHOULD HAVE SEEN THEM KICKING ACAPULCO GOLD.

I was talking recently to a member of one of America's top acid-rock bands, who had just returned from England.

"Hey, man, the English run a tight scene. Too literary."

"Too literary?"

"Yeah, man. Always analyzing and rapping about books. They even do the same thing with grass. The head trip."

"Well, I think that's great of Britain. The trouble with our hippies is, they aren't connected. Rootless. Turned on, but not tuned in. The acidheads would move further if they hooked up with their past. You know, the psychedelic experience has been around for a few thousand years before Haight-Ashbury. And

the English are the original hippies. They've been writing about it for three hundred years."

"No, man, that history thing isn't where it's at. It's a hang-up. Freak out! That's the boss trip. Blow your mind. Pow! Zap! . . ."

It's a curious fact that the American psychedelic movement is almost completely a British import. LSD. Pounds, shillings and pence.

AND THE HIGHS OF THE HEADS SEE THE WORLD TURNING ON.

Consider the lineage. The key architect of the revolution is a British psychiatrist named Humphrey Osmond. Who? He invented the term *psychedelic.* Humphrey? He turned on Aldous Huxley and Gerald Heard. Doctor Osmond? Along with Abram Hofer (a brilliant Canadian neurologist), he first demonstrated the benefits of LSD with hopeless alcoholics. Humphrey Osmond? He published the first papers suggesting that psychedelic drugs could produce a transcendental experience.

Doctor Humphrey Osmond is indeed a quiet, wise, compassionate Englishman. A humorous, thoughtful, scholarly scientist. A head of his time. Shrewd. Historical-political overview. Broad philosophic perspective on events about which American psychiatrists don't have a clue.

In 20 years of furious fulmination, America has yet to produce a psychiatrist who can say, with Osmond, "Calm down, it's been happening for millennia and it's inevitable and it's all right. Read your Jung, young man."

And thank you, Evans-Wentz and Arthur Waley, for Aldous Huxley. Aldous had been rummaging diligently for some 40 years through biology, physics, literature, philosophy, Vedanta, looking myopically through his magnifying glass for that central key-code that had gotten misplaced, and then Humphrey Osmond turned him on with mescaline and ushered him through the doors of perception, and Aldous laughed and exulted for the remaining years of his new life, chuckling about gratuitous grace.

And on the morning of November 22, 1963 (the last, dark day of our young President, himself a head), when Aldous Huxley heard the Tibetan whisper from his tissues that his time had come, O nobly born, to seek new levels of reality, your ego and the Aldous Huxley game are about to cease, he wrote on a piece of paper "LSD" and spent the last eight hours of his life on the eternal high wire, dying, smiling, just as he had described the smiling death of the old grandmother on his utopian *Island*.

And thank you, William Blake and A. A. Orage, for Alan Watts, mischievous Zen master, lyric Anglican priest (high church), source, inspiration and guide (although most of them don't know it) for San Francisco's flower children. Alan Watts lives on a retired ferryboat in Sauselito, a French Riviera fishing village across the bay from San Francisco. His looking-glass walls open out on a front lawn of shimmering water splashed by sea gull wings. From this undulating beach headquarters Alan Watts, Lord High Admiral of the Beat, has been teaching hip Zen, square Zen, Kyoto turn-on methods to a generation of Americans, and when acid hit San Francisco it was no acid-ent that it had a sweet Eastern flavor because Alan had been explaining Watts what.

There is, of course, high church psychedelic and low church.

Ken Kesey's acid-test-rock-and-roll-on-the-floor-freak-out is low church psychedelic, gutty, shouting, sawdust trail. Alan Watts is highest Anglican. Precise, ceremonial, serene, aesthetic, classic, aristocratic with a wink. The ancient rituals executed perfectly with a quiet twinkle in the eye. My understanding of marijuana and LSD is mainly due to my listening to and watching Alan.

Professional English isle watchers groan and demur when I praise the British cool. They cite grim horror stories of insular smugness. But can you imagine an American Senator or Cabinet member going to a scientific congress and talking about getting high like Christopher Mayhew, Member of Parliament and Her Majesty's First Lord of the Admiralty?

"I took the drug," said Cabinet member Christopher Mayhew to the assembled scientists, "because I am the old school friend of Doctor X [Humphrey Osmond]. He said he was coming over to England, and could I recommend him for a BBC Third Programme broadcast to describe his research work? I said, 'Don't go on sound radio. No one listens to that. Explain

about hallucinogens on television and give this stuff to me right in front of a film camera.'

"And the BBC quite rightly thought this a first-class idea for a program, and so did Doctor X. And he came down to my home in Surrey and in front of a film camera gave me, I think it would be four hundred milligrams of mescaline hydrochloride, sitting in my own armchair at home. Those are the circumstances of the experiment."

Oh, you say that Mr. Christ-bearer Mayhew is one eccentric Englishman, but he was not alone. In the same scientific psychedelic conference another Member of Parliament, the Honorable Donald Johnston, describes his psychedelic highs as "transcendental states; they put you in contact with some force or power with which you are normally out of contact in your everyday life. . . . Reverting finally to the 'significance of these states,' in my case not only did this curious state seem significant but it was significant, because the whole trend of my life did happen to alter. There is only one way in which a politician's trend of life can alter, and that is according to whether you lose elections or whether you win elections; and whereupon prior to this event [his psychedelic drug experience] ten years ago, I had spent my life losing every parliamentary election I fought, I have been fortunate enough to win elections since then. Otherwise I would not be claiming colleagueship with Christopher Mayhew.

"And I say now, even after five and a half years, that this was the most interesting and thought-provoking thing I have ever experienced in my life. And I say this even today, when the emotion, the vividness, has all worn off and only a kind of intellectual conviction remains. Not only winning elections but winning very close elections. Yes, this is something for you ladies and gentlemen to think about."

THERE'S A FOG UPON NEW DELHI WHEN MY FRIENDS LEAVE PSYCHEDELLY.

O.K. Can you imagine an American Senator, let's say Mr. Fulbright of Arkansas or Mr. Charles Percy of Illinois, attributing his election not to the wisdom of his voting constituents but to his having turned on?

Oh, but you say, that was in the 1950's, before the generals discovered that turned-on flower people won't go to war. To-day, you say, no politician would dare defend LSD or that greater vegetable men-ace, marijuana. You are almost right. In China, ecstasy is treason. In Russia, pleasure is anti-Communist. In Scandinavia, turning on disturbs the smooth-blonde-butter-bacon-fat-hush of Socialism. To an African dictator who has just gotten his hands on whiskey and machine guns, getting high is a colonial conspiracy. Fierce Nasser fears the gentle hashish more than Israeli jets. Senator Fulbright, the great liberal, allows puritan Harry Anslinger, director of our narcotics pogrom, to PUSH an international treaty through the U.S. Congress which prevents America from legalizing marijuana. And only in Eng-land would the following parliamentary debate take place in the year of our stoned-out-laughing God 1967:

HOUSE OF COMMONS
Friday, 28th July 1967
PARLIAMENTARY DEBATE
SOFT DRUGS

Mr. H. P. G. Channon (Southend West) : All sections of the House will agree that there is now abundant evidence that in the past few years there has been a vast increase in the use of drugs of all kinds in this country, and in particular by young people.

No Honorable Member has not at some time taken a soft drug, which can be something as minor as caffeine or tea, and few have not taken alcohol or nicotine at some time. These are the soft drugs, which are not socially unacceptable in this country.

The most difficult and controversial topic at the moment is the use of cannabis, or marijuana, by young people. This is where the law is most widely flouted. I would like the Honor-able Members to ask themselves, first, why these drugs are taken. In every generation there is a wish to rebel, first of all, against the standards of the previous generation. There is something of that in the use of cannabis. Young people still have too little realization of the dangers of all drugs. I was glad to see that the Secretary of State for Education and Science is to launch a bigger program on that in schools.

TRANSCENDENTAL TEA SHIRT, INSTANT MEDITATION, JOHN YOU BEEN A NAUGHTY GEORGE—YOU LET YOUR TRIPS GROW MOD.

Above all, however, there is a feeling that those who are a little older are hypocritical, particularly about cannabis. Young people consider, rightly or wrongly, that they are persecuted for a harmless pleasure, while adults freely use nicotine, which probably leads to cancer, and alcohol, and we all know tragic cases of alcoholism. Young people also feel that it is hypocritical for the state to make vast sums of money, particularly out of tobacco, and that the state's moral values are wrong. I do not defend or condone this attitude, but it is understandable.

The argument has come to a head in recent months because there is no doubt that the number of young people smoking cannabis has increased. It was also brought to a head by an advertisement in the Times *this week in which it was alleged by many distinguished people, including medical people and the Beatles, that the law against cannabis at the moment is "immoral in principle and unworkable in practice."*

THEY'RE LEAVING HOME. BYE-BYE.

With the latter half of that statement I am beginning to agree. I think that the law is becoming increasingly unworkable in practice. I do not know whether the House realizes how many respectable young people indulge in the practice. I am not talking about the lower strata, the people who are so distressed that they have no other form of relief than marijuana. I fear that there are large numbers of respectable people with good jobs, or students, who are taking the drugs, and they represent an intelligent section of our society. For them repression is not enough. They must be convinced as well as repressed, if repression is the right step.

YOUNG PEOPLE WILL GO ON.

I want to see the problem solved, because I am certain that young people will go on using the drug unless they can be convinced intellectually that it has the dangerous dangers which it is widely believed to possess. I am told that we have the mildest kind of marijuana in Britain and that there is a grave danger in the future that we shall have adulterated marijuana, maybe mixed with heroin or opium, if this situation is allowed to slide much longer.

PARLIAMENT IS SITTING; PRETTY LITTLE MALICEMEN IN A ROW.

I very much doubt whether the law is the best way to control human behavior of this kind. I believe that it must be inquired into, and I would see some advantages if it were possible to control this drug as alcohol is controlled—with far stricter control of those under eighteen who take the drug. There will have to be far stricter control, for example, of people who drive cars while under the influence of this drug.

What alarms me about this, as with so many social problems, is that it has been creeping up on us for some time, almost unnoticed, until suddenly it has begun to snowball. The problem has reached a crucial point. Many people talk about the generation gap. That has always existed. Nevertheless, there is something in that argument today. I am sure the gap between the generations is greater than it was ten years ago, because I find that so many young people suspect our generation of hypocrisy.

Mr. Tom Driberg (Barking): I shall speak only briefly, in order to allow my Honorable friend Minister of State to answer the debate and to any other Honorable Member who may wish to speak. The debate will have been of great use if it leads to the further research and action which the Honorable Member for Southend West [Mr. Channon] suggested, and I congratulate him on having raised this hotly topical subject.

He referred to the [legalize pot] advertisement in the Times
*of last Monday. I was one of the only two Members of this
House who signed it and would not have done so if I had not
been in general agreement with what was said. There have been
criticisms of the advertisement in the* Times, *but I do not think
that such people as Dr. Stafford-Clark, Dr. Antony Storr, and
other doctors and scientists, including the two Nóbel Prize win-
ners, would have signed it if this had been a completely irresponsible thing to do.*

*Mr. Marcus Lipton (Brixton): The Honorable Member for
Southend West [Mr. Channon] has served a very useful purpose in raising this difficult and topical subject today. I find
myself in a large measure of agreement with the aims of this
committee, about which the general public do not know very
much. It should be given some advertisement.*

*We should also like to know when this committee started to
discuss the problem of cannabis, how often it meets and when it
is likely to report. Who is sitting on it? Whose opinions are we
asked to accept on this? It is a vitally important thing that
whatever this committee reports should be accepted by the
general public, particularly by the younger generation. It is no
use using Victorian language hoping to convince the younger
generation.*

SHAKING BACON CHOKING SMOKERS, DO YOU THINK THE *KIDS* WILL
VOTE *FOR YOU?*

*Miss Alice Bacon, Minister of State, Home Office: I have only
a few minutes and cannot give way.*

*Views have been given this morning about cannabis. It would
be entirely mad for the government to relax the laws without
more information to be obtained by the committee. It has been
said in this morning's newspapers that in Birmingham a great
many people who take heroin started with cannabis. Ninety-
seven percent of the heroin addicts known to the Home Office
have a previous history of cannabis taking.*

Mr. Driberg: And of alcohol.

Miss Bacon: The government would be mad, apart from the

international conventions of which we are a part, to relax these restrictions.

I believe that at the present time we are in danger in this country. I am not speaking only of cannabis but also of some other drugs which have been mentioned, particularly LSD—of some people misleading young people by not only taking drugs themselves but trying to influence the minds of young people and encourage them to take drugs. I do not often read the Queen, *but I was at the hairdresser's yesterday. [Honorable Members: "Hear, hear."] This magazine was passed to me to while away the time when I was under the hair dryer. There is a very long article in it called "The Love Generation," with statements by various people who are pop singers and managers of pop singers. I was horrified at some of the things I read in it. For instance, Paul McCartney says, among other things:*

> *God is in everything. God is in the space between us. God is in that table in front of you. God is everything and everywhere and everyone.*
>
> *It just happens that I realized all this through acid [LSD], but it could have been done through anything. It really doesn't matter how I made it. . . . The final result is all that counts.*

Mr. Channon: Is the Honorable lady quoting prominent people in favor of drug taking? It is terribly dangerous to quote people like that when we are against drug taking.

Mr. Driberg: He [Paul McCartney] is a very good man.

KIDS NEVER LISTEN TO THEM—THEY KNOW THAT THEY'RE THE FOOLS.

Miss Bacon: I am illustrating the argument. The Honorable Member raised this question this morning and, running through his speech, I thought I detected a sort of feeling that we should relax on cannabis. Maybe I am wrong, but if he does not want any publicity to be given at all, this debate should not have taken place this morning.

The manager of the Beatles said in this article that there is a new mood in the country and:

"This new mood has originated from hallucinatory drugs, and I am wholeheartedly on its side."

This may sound amusing to Honorable Members, but young people take quite seriously what pop stars say. What sort of society will we create if everyone wants to escape from reality?

Mr. Driberg: They want to escape from this horrible society we have created.

Miss Bacon: Today there are those who see in society's attitude to drug taking the opportunity for questioning traditional values and self-judgments of all kinds and for advocating aims and conduct going far beyond the "kicks" and pleasures of a few pills. For them drug taking is a way—the way—of life to which they beckon the impressionable, the curious, the frustrated, and the demoralized. Insidiously or openly, wittingly or unwittingly, the young are being taught the paraphernalia of psychedelic experience, and the catch phrases of drug cults.

HAIRDRESSER WISHWIFE ALCOHOLIC ALICE—GIRL YOU BEEN A NAUGHTY BOY. YOU LET YOUR ROCK STARS DOWN.

This seems to be the real challenge of soft drugs, and it is growing. The government believes that it is time for responsible influences to check the trend. It is time to make clear that teen-age drug taking is ill-advised, if not dangerous to personality and health. It is time to rebut the claim of those who profess to make mystics out of the immature. This is a challenge which all sections of society must take up. The government are resolved to do their part.

Thank you, Mr. Channon, Mr. Driberg and Mr. Lipton, for the light and humor in these gloomy times. May your constituents reach voting age and continue to turn you on and turn your Honorable enemies out.

BUT THE KIDS ON THE THRILL SEE THE SUN GOING ON.

And then there is Ronald Laing, turned-on, wry Scottish shaman.

One day in 1964 I received a phone call from a British psychiatrist visiting New York. Mentioned Allen Ginsberg.

Wanted to come to visit. O.K. He'd arrive on the noon train tomorrow. Name of Ronald Laing.

When he phoned from the train station, I groaned. Another dreary, platitudinous psychiatrist. He walked into the kitchen, and we stood looking at each other. He was solid brown tweed with a flicker of gold.

We sat at the table, ate a sandwich, drank wine. I told him that medical-therapeutic talk about LSD was a fake. I was interested only in the mystic aspects of the drug.

His move.

He said that the only doctor who could heal was the one who understood the shamanic, witchcraft mystery of medicine.

Ronald Laing took off his coat and loosened his tie.

AND THE HEADS IN HIS ISLE SEE THE WORLD TURNING ON.

After a bit he said he knew an interesting game. Did I want to play it?

We took off our shoes and stood in the space between the kitchen sink and the table.

The point of this game is to move your hands and your body without talking.

We began to spar, karate style, moving in between each other's guard.

Do we have to spar?

A shrug.

Our hands changed into a dance. Paired sculpturing of air, molded liquid forms, now moving slowly, then whirling. My eyes were riveted to his eyes. I was gone. Spun out of the kitchen at Millbrook, spun out of time. Stoned high in a Sufi ballet. We were two organisms from different planets—communicating. I was an Eskimo on an ice floe. He was a visiting explorer. We were exchanging the hard-core information about life, our tribe, the mystery. We were two animals of different species, of the same species, of the same litter, from separate ages.

We were sitting on the floor in the lotus position, arms, hands, weaving. The dialogue lasted for an hour Greenwich time. A dozen people had walked in, watched and left the kitchen. My son and some friends came home from school, glanced at the two seated forms, made lunch and left. "My dad and his friends are potty."

We opened our eyes. It was dark. Time to catch the train back to New York.

Six months later, in Alex Trocchi's London nerve-pulse heart chamber, people sitting around taking the Trocchi trip. Door opens. Ronnie Laing enters. Sits on mattress. Begins to describe some Tantric sex rituals that an old schizophrenic patient-cum-guru had passed on to him. Soft Scot burr. Exquisite psychedelic poetry. He had all our heads in his graceful hands. Especially the women.

WHY DON'T WE SINK THIS WRONG ALL TOGETHER? OPEN OUR HEARTS AND LET THE VISION COME?

You will not find on this planet a more fascinating man than Ronald Laing. A *pontifex*. A bridge builder between worlds. As a straight psychiatric researcher he casually turns out sophisticated, penetrating books about the social meaning of mental illness. Turns on that dreariest of professions with graceful strokes. An elegant hippy. Shrewd Eden-burg observations. Academic poise. He is tuned in to Eastern philosophy, English poetry. *Magister ludi.* He weaves science-religion-art-experience into the slickest bead game of our time.

YOUR MOTHER SHOULD FLOW, YOUR GURU SHOULD KNOW.

Historical note: On December 31, 1600, Queen Elizabeth granted a charter to the English East India Company. The aim of the game was to bring back peppers and spices of the East. The fabled turn-on vegetables. This charter granted over 350 years ago has had more effect on the psychedelic revolution of the 1960's than Sandoz Laboratories and its lysergic discoveries. Without the East India expedition LSD would be a pharmacological curiosity.

It happened like this. From 1600 to 1946 several hundred

thousand Englishmen—soldiers, administrators, scholars—took a trip to India. They went there to mind a colony, but many of them got their minds colonized by smiling Krishna, the aphrodisiac love god. The impact of a visit to India is psychedelic. You are flipped out of your space-time identity. Indian life unfolds before you a million-flowered-person-vine-serpent coil of life ancient, wrinkled, dancing, starving, laughing, sick, swarming, inconceivable, unreasonable, mocking, singing-multiheaded, laughing God dance.

And the English in India got turned on. Even today the tourist who strays from the deluxe plastic path and wanders into the villages will be offered bhang, charras, ganga, attar, some one of a thousand ways the Indians prepare hemp.

OH, WE'VE GOT ALL THE GOOROOS AN' WE'VE GOT LOVELY TABOOS, TOO.

I spent a winter once in a little hut near the Himalayan snow peaks. Before his weekly hike to the village to shop, my Moslem cook would ask, "Two attar?" and I'd nod and give him an extra dollar, and he'd come back with two sticks, as long as your little finger, of the best hashish that ever stoned out a Mongul emperor, and I'd give him one and he'd grin. It was rolled into a hard, resinous stick by hand and smoked by all the farmers, and you can bet that this little weekly ceremony—me and my smiling cook—had been acted out for 300 years by every Englishman in India who had ears to listen and eyes to see what was happening.

And after you turn on with hashish you can tune in to the incredible sensuous hit of India and the myriad mystic mosaic of India, and you can read the Vedas and Vedantas in your own tissues and understand.

Hundreds of thousands of Englishmen returned home to the island turned around by the Indian consciousness. Britannia ruled the plains, but India copped the rulers' brains. The intellectual fabric of England is indelibly imprinted with the undulating madras, paisley design.

MEHER BABA HOOVER CLIMBING UP THE DOLLAR TOWER.

And this accounts for the fact that English intellectuals never swallowed French rationalism, the bitter gaul of mind spinning out its chess moves to the inevitable end of the head-trip-existential despair. Reason is absurd but energy-maya-prana consciousness is not absurd because it moves, merges, copulates, smiles, and lovingly swallows up the mind. Few French intellectuals grasped this and the few that did, like René Daumal and Baudelaire, were Sanskrit scholars and hashish heads.

You recall that while Jules Verne was writing about clanking mechanical trips 1,000 leagues "down," H. G. Wells, a visionary Englishman, saw mind at the end of its tether and predicted quite accurately that mankind would mutate into two different species—the gentle flower people living in the sun and the machine people living underground.

And E. M. Forster made the passage to India, and Charles Dodgson tripped with mushroom-eating Alice, Jonathan Swift tripped with Gulliver, James Joyce tripped with Bloom and Earwicker, John Bunyan with the Christian Pilgrim, J. R. R. Tolkien with his elves, and how about Alistair Crowley and Conan Doyle.

Britannia—you are a nation of inveterate trippers, heads and stoned visionaries!

It was unavoidable that the first great psychedelic novel would be written by someone with a name like John Fowles. *The Magus.* Not since I read Joyce's *Ulysses* in 1941 have I experienced that special epic-mystery excitement from a book. *The Magus* raises the basic ontological questions, confronts the ancient, divine mystery and backs away from the riddle with the exact balance of reverence and humor. At Millbrook we use *The Magus* as psychochemical litmus paper. Those readers who report boredom just haven't made our trip.

And then come the Beatles, hoping to take us away.

Obeisances and profound gratitude to you, inspired revealers of the great vibration.

The Four Evangelists!

Are you meaning St. Paul and St. John and St. George? I mean now, thank all, the four of them and the roar of them that drays that stray in the mist, and old St. Ringo along with them. And George Martin. And the Rolling Stones.

Rosemary and I spent the summer of '67 in a tepee on Ecstasy Hill in Millbrook, devoting an hour or two each day to getting high and listening to a portable record player spin the new testaments according to Sergeant Pepper and their Satanic Majesties. It's all there.

How clever and unexpected and yet typical of God to send his message this time through the electric instruments of four men from Liverpool and the Holy Rollers.

IF THE FUN DON'T COME, YOU FIND THE MAN A' STANDING ON THE HARDWAR PLAIN.

Beloved gurus of Liverpool, I'm four you. I've got nothing to say that you haven't said briefer, cleaner, stronger.

It was as inevitable that George Harrison would go to India as it was that Elvis Presley would go to Hollywood and that Mick Jagger and Keith Richards would write in a prison cell holy hymns forgiving their jailers.

To future social historians I humbly suggest that the spiritual cord that holds our civilization from suicide can be traced from the Himalayan forests where Vedic philosophers drank soma, down the Ganja, through the Suez by P. and O. and over to Liverpool.

My fellow Americans, psychedelicists, hippies, flowerheads, monks, nuns, searchers, trippers, I humbly suggest that to find God we have to learn to speak English. Our DNA code seems to.*

---

* This article is the first of a two-part series. In the second essay the author will demonstrate on the basis of philological, anthropological and historical evidence that the literary-spiritual soul of the English language is actually Celtic.

7

She Comes in Colors*

On a sunny Saturday afternoon in 1960, beside the swimming pool of his rented summer villa in Cuernavaca, a thirty-nine-year-old American ate a handful of odd-looking mushrooms he'd bought from the witch doctor of a nearby village. Within minutes, he recalled later, he felt himself "being swept over the edge of a sensory Niagara into a maelstrom of transcendental visions and hallucinations. The next 5 hours could be described in many extravagant metaphors, but it was above all and without question the deepest religious experience of my life." The implications of that fateful first communion are as yet unmeasured; that they are both far-reaching and profound, however, is generally conceded—for the fungi were the legendary "sacred mushrooms" that have since become known, and feared by many, as one of the psychedelic (literally, mind-manifesting) chemicals that have created a national fad among the nation's young and a scandal in the press. The American was a Harvard psychotherapist named Timothy Leary, who has since found himself transmogrified from scientist and researcher into

---

* Reprinted from the September 1966 issue of *Playboy* magazine. Copyright © 1966 by HMH Publishing Company, Inc. If this interview had been conducted for *Sports Illustrated*, the conscientious interviewee would naturally consider the question, How LSD Can Raise Your Batting Average. Considerable thought was given to the title of this chapter. To reflect concisely the dilemma of the interviewee Paul Krassner suggested: "Collecting Orgasms for Fun and Profit." Michael Hollingshead contributed: "Commonsensual Advice for Serious Playboys." Darlene chipped in with: "LSD for Bunnies and Playboys." The version selected (for the first edition) was offered by Rosemary Leary, with admiring thanks to the Rolling Stones.

progenitor and high priest of a revolutionary movement spawned, not by an idea but by a substance that's been called "the spiritual equivalent of the hydrogen bomb."

Few men, in their youth, would have seemed less likely to emerge as a religious leader, let alone as a rebel with a cause. At the age of nineteen, Leary distressed his Roman Catholic mother by abandoning Holy Cross two years before graduation ("the scholastic approach to religion didn't turn me on"), then affronted his father, a retired Army career officer, by walking out of West Point after 18 months ("my interests were philosophic rather than militaristic"). Not until he transferred to the University of Alabama did he begin to settle down academically —to work for his B.A. in psychology. On graduation in 1942 he enlisted as an Army psychologist, served in a Pennsylvania hospital until the end of the war, then resumed his schooling and earned his Ph.D. at the University of California at Berkeley. Acquiring both eminence and enemies with his first major jobs—as director of Oakland's progressive Kaiser Foundation Hospital and as an assistant professor at UC's School of Medicine in San Francisco—Leary began to display the courage and sometimes rash iconoclasm that have since marked every phase of his checkered career. Contending that traditional psychiatric methods were hurting as many patients as they helped, he resigned in 1958 and signed up as a lecturer on clinical psychology at Harvard. There he began to evolve and enunciate the theory of social interplay and personal behavior as so many stylized games, since popularized by Dr. Eric Berne in his best-selling book Games People Play, *and to both preach and practice the effective but unconventional new psychiatric research technique of sending his students to study emotional problems such as alcoholism where they germinate, rather than in the textbook or the laboratory.*

At the time, predictably enough, few of these novel notions went over very well with Leary's hidebound colleagues. But their rumblings of skepticism rose to a chorus of outrage when Leary returned to Harvard in 1960 from his pioneering voyage into inner space—beside the swimming pool in Cuernavaca—to begin experimenting on himself, his associates and hundreds of volunteer subjects with measured doses of psilocybin, the chemical derivative of the sacred mushrooms. Vowing "to dedicate the rest of my life as a psychologist to the systematic exploration of this new instrument," he and his rapidly multiplying followers began to turn on with the other psychedelics: morning-glory seeds, nutmeg, marijuana, peyote, mescaline—and a colorless, odorless, tasteless but incredibly potent laboratory compound called LSD 25, first synthesized in 1938 by a Swiss biochemist seeking a pain-killer for migraine headaches. A hundred times stronger than psilocybin, LSD sent its hallucinated users on multihued, multileveled roller-coaster rides so spectacular that it soon became Leary's primary tool for research. And as word began to circulate about the fantastic, phantasmagorical "trips" taken by his students, it soon became a clandestine campus kick and by 1962 had become an underground cult among the young avant-garde from London to Los Angeles.

By 1963 it had also become something of an embarrassment to Harvard, however, which "regretfully" dismissed Leary, and his colleague Dr. Richard Alpert in order to stem the rising tide of avid undergraduate interest in the drug. Undaunted, they organized a privately financed research group called the International Foundation for Internal Freedom (IFIF), and set up a psychedelic study center in Zihuatanejo, Mexico, but before they could resume full-scale LSD sessions, the Mexican government stepped in, anticipating adverse popular reaction, and demanded that they leave the country.

Leary had now become not only the messiah but the martyr of the psychedelic movement. But soon afterward came a dramatic eleventh-hour reprieve from a young New York millionaire named William Hitchcock, a veteran LSD voyager who believed in the importance of Leary's work—by now a mission—and toward that end turned over to him a rambling mansion on his 4,000-acre estate in Millbrook, New York, which has since become not only Leary's home and headquarters but also a kind of shrine and sanctuary for psychedelic pilgrims from all over *the world. On April 16, 1966, it also became a target for further harassment by what Leary calls "the forces of middle-aged, middle-class authority." Late that night, a squad of Dutchess County police descended on the place, searched it from top to bottom, found a minute quantity of marijuana, and arrested four people —including Leary. If convicted, he could be fined heavily and sent to prison for 16 years. Already appealing another conviction, Leary had been arrested in Laredo the previous December as he was about to enter Mexico for a vacation, when customs officials searched his car and found a half ounce of marijuana in the possession of his eighteen-year-old daughter. Despite his claim that the drug was for scientific and sacramental use in the furtherance of his work and his spiritual beliefs (as a practicing Hindu), he was fined $30,000 and sentenced to 30 years in prison for transporting marijuana and failing to pay the federal marijuana tax.*

In the months since then, the LSD controversy has continued to escalate along with Leary's notoriety—spurred by a spate of headline stories about psychedelic psychoses, dire warnings of "instant insanity" from police and public health officials, and pious editorials inveighing against the evils of the drug. In May and June, two Senate subcommittees conducted widely publicized public hearings on LSD, and three states—California, Nevada and New Jersey—enacted laws prohibiting its illicit use, possession, distribution or manufacture. With a ringing appeal for still more stringent legislation on a federal level, Ronald Reagan even dragged the issue into his successful campaign for the Republican gubernatorial nomination in California.

It was amid this mounting outcry against the drug that Playboy *asked Dr. Leary to present his side of the psychedelic story— and to answer a few pertinent questions about its putative promise and its alleged perils. Consenting readily, he invited us to visit him in Millbrook, where we found him a few days later reciting Hindu morning prayers with a group of guests in the kitchen of the 64-room mansion. He greeted us warmly and led the way to a third-floor library. Instead of sitting down in one of the room's well-worn easy chairs, he crossed the room, stepped out of an open window onto a tin roof over a second-floor bay window, and proceeded to stretch out on a double-width mattress a few feet from the edge. While we made ourself comfortable at the other end of the mattress, he opened his shirt to the warm summer sun, propped his bare feet against the shingles, looked down at the mansion's vast rolling meadow of a lawn, listened for a moment to the song of a chickadee in the branches of a tree nearby, and then turned, ready for our first question.*

PLAYBOY: How many times have you used LSD, Dr. Leary?

LEARY: Up to this moment, I've had 311 psychedelic sessions.

PLAYBOY: What do you think it's done for you—and to you?

LEARY: That's difficult to answer easily. Let me say this: I was thirty-nine when I had my first psychedelic experience. At that time, I was a middle-aged man involved in the middle-aged process of dying. My joy in life, my sensual openness, my creativity were all sliding downhill. Since that time, six years ago, my life has been renewed in almost every dimension. Most of my colleagues at the University of California and at Harvard, of course, feel that I've become an eccentric and a kook. I would estimate that fewer than 15 percent of my professional colleagues understand and support what I'm doing. The ones who do, as you might expect, tend to be among the younger psychologists. If you know a person's age, you know what he's going to think and feel about LSD. Psychedelic drugs are the medium of the young. As you move up the age scale into the thirties, forties and fifties, fewer and fewer people are open to the possibilities that these chemicals offer.

PLAYBOY: Why is that?

LEARY: To the person over thirty-five or forty, the word "drug" means one of two things: doctor-disease or dope fiend-crime. Nothing you can say to a person who has this neurological fix on the word "drug" is going to change his mind. He's frozen like a Pavlovian dog to this conditioned reflex. To people under twenty-five, on the other hand, the word "drug" refers to a wide range of mind benders running from alcohol, energizers and stupefiers to marijuana and the other psychedelic drugs. To middle-aged America, it may be synonymous with instant insanity, but to most Americans under twenty-five, the psychedelic drug means ecstasy, sensual unfolding, religious experience, revelation, illumination, contact with nature. There's hardly a teen-ager or young person in the United States today who doesn't know at least one person who has had a good experience with marijuana or LSD. The horizons of the current younger generation, in terms of expanded consciousness, are light-years beyond those of their parents. The breakthrough has occurred; there's no going back. The psychedelic battle is won.

PLAYBOY: What do you say to the standard charge that LSD is too powerful and dangerous to entrust to the young?

LEARY: Well, none of us yet knows exactly how LSD can be used for the growth and benefit of the human being. It is a powerful releaser of energy as yet not fully understood. But if I'm confronted with the possibility that a fifteen-year-old or a fifty-year-old is going to use a new form of energy that he doesn't understand, I'll back the fifteen-year-old every time. Why? Because a fifteen-year-old is going to use a new form of energy to have fun, to intensify sensation, to make love, for curiosity, for personal growth. Many fifty-year-olds have lost their curiosity, have lost their ability to make love, have dulled their openness to new sensations, and would use any form of new energy for power, control and warfare. So it doesn't concern me at all that young people are taking time out from the educational and occupational assembly lines to experiment with consciousness, to dabble with new forms of experience and artistic expression. The present generation under the age of twenty-five is the wisest and holiest generation that the human race has ever seen. And by God, instead of lamenting, derogating and imprisoning them, we should support them, listen to them and turn on with them.

PLAYBOY: If we wanted to take you up on that last suggestion, how would we go about it?

LEARY: Find a beloved friend who knows where to get LSD

and how to run a session, or find a trusted and experienced LSD voyager to guide you on a trip.

PLAYBOY: Is it necessary to have a guide?

LEARY: Yes. Unless you have an experienced guide—at least for your first 10 or 15 sessions—it would be confusing.

PLAYBOY: What if a person can't find either a guide or a source of LSD among his friends? Where does he go?

LEARY: LSD is against the law, and I certainly would not advise anyone to violate the law. I will say this, however: Throughout human history, men who have wanted to expand their consciousness, to find deeper meaning inside themselves, have been able to do it if they were willing to commit the time and energy to do so. In other times and countries, men would walk barefooted 2,000 miles to find spiritual teachers who would turn them on to Buddha, Mohammed or Ramakrishna.

PLAYBOY: If you can't say where one could buy LSD, can you tell us the formula for making it? We understand it can be synthesized in any well-equipped chemical laboratory.

LEARY: That's true. But it would be irresponsible of me to reveal it. The unauthorized manufacture of LSD is now against the law.

PLAYBOY: Assuming you can get it, how do you take it? Can it be injected, or is it mostly just swallowed in a sugar cube?

LEARY: It can be injected or it can come in the form of powder or pills or in a solution, which is odorless, tasteless and colorless. In any case, you're dealing with a very minute quantity. One hundred micrograms is a moderate dose.

PLAYBOY: For a session lasting how long?

LEARY: Eight to twelve hours.

PLAYBOY: What's it like? What happens to you?

LEARY: If we're speaking in a general way, what happens to everyone is the experience of incredible acceleration and intensification of all senses and of all mental processes—which can be very confusing if you're not prepared for it. Around a thousand million signals fire off in your brain every second; during any second in an LSD session, you find yourself tuned in on thousands of these messages that ordinarily you don't register consciously. And you may be getting an incredible number of simultaneous messages from different parts of your body. Since you're not used to this, it can lead to incredible ecstasy or it can lead to confusion. Some people are freaked by this Niagara of sensory input. Instead of having just one or two or three things happening in tidy sequence, you're suddenly flooded by hundreds of lights and colors and sensations and images, and you can get quite lost.

You sense a strange powerful force beginning to unloose and radiate through your body. In normal perception, we are aware of static symbols. But as the LSD effect takes hold, everything begins to *move,* and this relentless, impersonal, slowly swelling movement will continue through the several hours of the session. It's as though for all of your normal waking life you have been caught in a still photograph, in an awkward, stereotyped posture; suddenly the show comes alive, balloons out to several dimensions and becomes irradiated with color and energy.

The first thing you notice is an incredible enhancement of sensory awareness. Take the sense of sight. LSD vision is to normal vision as normal vision is to the picture on a badly tuned television set. Under LSD, it's as though you have microscopes up to your eyes, in which you see jewellike, radiant details of anything your eye falls upon. You are really seeing for the first time—not static, symbolic perception of learned things, but patterns of light bouncing off the objects around you and hurtling at the speed of light into the mosaic of rods and cones in the retina of your eye. Everything seems alive. Everything *is* alive, beaming diamond-bright light waves into your retina.

PLAYBOY: Is the sense of hearing similarly intensified?

LEARY: Tremendously. Ordinarily we hear just isolated sounds: the rings of a telephone, the sound of somebody's words. But when you turn on with LSD, the organ of Corti in your inner ear becomes a trembling membrane seething with tattoos of sound waves. The vibrations seem to penetrate deep inside you, swell and burst there. You hear one note of a Bach sonata, and it hangs there, glittering, pulsating, for an endless length of time, while you slowly orbit around it. Then, hundreds of years later, comes the second note of the sonata, and again, for hundreds of years, you slowly drift around the two notes, observing the harmony and the discords, and reflecting on the history of music.

But when your nervous system is turned on with LSD, and all the wires are flashing, the senses begin to overlap and merge. You not only hear but *see* the music emerging from the speaker system—like dancing particles, like squirming curls of toothpaste. You actually *see* the sound in multicolored patterns while you're hearing it. At the same time, you *are* the sound, you are the note, you are the string of the violin or the piano. And every one of your organs is pulsating and having orgasms in rhythm with it.

PLAYBOY: What happens to the sense of taste?

LEARY: Taste is intensified, too, although normally you won't feel like eating during an LSD session, any more than you feel like eating when you take your first solo at the controls of a supersonic jet. Although if you eat after a session, there is an appreciation of all the particular qualities of food—its texture and resiliency and viscosity—such as we are not conscious of in a normal state of awareness.

PLAYBOY: How about the sense of smell?

LEARY: This is one of the most overwhelming aspects of an LSD experience. It seems as though for the first time you are breathing life, and you remember with amusement and distaste that plastic, odorless, artificial gas that you used to consider air. During the LSD experience, you discover that you're actually inhaling an atmosphere composed of millions of microscopic strands of olfactory ticker tape, exploding in your nostrils with ecstatic meaning. When you sit across the room from a woman during an LSD session, you're aware of thousands of penetrating chemical messages floating from her through the air into your sensory center: a symphony of a thousand odors that all of us exude at every moment—the shampoo she uses, her cologne, her sweat, the exhaust and discharge from her digestive system, her sexual perfume, the fragrance of her clothing—grenades of eroticism exploding in the olfactory cell.

PLAYBOY: Does the sense of touch become equally erotic?

LEARY: Touch becomes electric as well as erotic. I remember a moment during one session in which Rosemary leaned over and lightly touched the palm of my hand with her finger. Immediately a hundred thousand end cells in my hand exploded in soft orgasm. Ecstatic energies pulsated up my arms and rocketed into my brain, where another hundred thousand cells softly exploded in pure, delicate pleasure. The distance between my wife's finger and the palm of my hand was about 50 miles of space, filled with cotton candy, infiltrated with thousands of silver wires hurtling energy back and forth. Wave after waver of exquisite energy pulsed from her finger. Wave upon wave of ethereal tissue rapture—delicate, shuddering—coursed back and forth from her finger to my palm.

PLAYBOY: And this rapture was erotic?

LEARY: Transcendentally. An enormous amount of energy from every fiber of your body is released under LSD—most especially including sexual energy. There is no question that LSD is the most powerful aphrodisiac ever discovered by man.

PLAYBOY: Would you elaborate?

LEARY: I'm saying simply that sex under LSD becomes miraculously enhanced and intensified. I don't mean that it simply generates genital energy. It doesn't automatically produce a longer erection. Rather, it increases your sensitivity a thousand percent. Let me put it this way: Compared with sex under LSD, the way you've been making love—no matter how ecstatic the pleasure you think you get from it—is like making love to a department-store-window dummy. In sensory and cellular communion on LSD, you may spend a half hour making love with eyeballs, another half hour making love with breath. As you spin through a thousand sensory and cellular organic changes, she does, too. Ordinarily, sexual communication involves one's own chemicals, pressure and interactions of a very localized nature—in what the psychologists call the erogenous zones. A vulgar, dirty concept, I think. When you're making love under LSD, it's as though every cell in your body—and you have trillions—is making love with every cell in her body. Your hand doesn't caress her skin but sinks down into and merges with ancient dynamos of ecstasy within her.

PLAYBOY: How often have you made love under the influence of LSD?

LEARY: Every time I've taken it. In fact, that is what the LSD experience is all about. Merging, yielding, flowing, union, communion. It's all lovemaking. You make love with candlelight, with sound waves from a record player, with a bowl of fruit on the table, with the trees. You're in pulsating harmony with all the energy around you.

PLAYBOY: Including that of a woman?

LEARY: The three inevitable goals of the LSD session are to discover and make love with God, to discover and make love with yourself, and to discover and make love with a woman. You can't make it with yourself unless you've made it with the timeless energy process around you, and you can't make it with a woman until you've made it with yourself. The natural and obvious way to take LSD is with a member of the opposite sex, and an LSD session that does not involve an ultimate merging with a person of the opposite sex isn't really complete. One of the great purposes of an LSD session is sexual union. The more expanded your consciousness—the farther out you can move beyond your mind—the deeper, the richer, the longer and more meaningful your sexual communion.

PLAYBOY: We've heard about sessions in which couples make love for hours on end, to the point of exhaustion, but never seem to reach exhaustion. Is this true?

LEARY: Yup.

PLAYBOY: Can you describe the sensation of an orgasm under LSD?

LEARY: Only the most reckless poet would attempt that. I have to say to you, "What does one say to a little child?" The child asks, "Daddy, what is sex like?" and you try to describe it, and then the little child says, "Well, is it fun like the circus?" and you say, "Well, not exactly like that." And the child says, "Is it fun like chocolate ice cream?" and you say, "Well, it's like that but much, much *more* than that." And the child says, "Is it fun like the roller coaster, then?" and you say, "Well, that's part of it, but it's even more than that." In short, I can't tell you what it's like, because it's not like anything that's ever happened to you—and there aren't words adequate to describe it, anyway. You won't know what it's like until you try it yourself and then I won't *need* to tell you.

PLAYBOY: We've heard that some women who ordinarily have difficulty achieving orgasm find themselves capable of multiple orgasms under LSD. Is that true?

LEARY: In a carefully prepared, loving LSD session, a woman can have several hundred orgasms.

PLAYBOY: Several *hundred?*

LEARY: Yes. Several hundred.

PLAYBOY: What about a man?

LEARY: This preoccupation with the number of orgasms is a hang-up for many men and women. It's as crude and vulgar a concept as wondering how much she paid for the negligee.

PLAYBOY: Still, there must be some sort of physiological comparison. If a woman can have several hundred orgasms, how many can a man have under optimum conditions?

LEARY: It would depend entirely on the amount of sexual— and psychedelic—experience the man has had. I can speak only for myself and about my own experience. I can only compare what I was with what I am now. In the last six years, my openness to, my responsiveness to, my participation in every form of sensory expression, has multiplied a *thousandfold*.

PLAYBOY: This aspect of LSD has been hinted at privately but never spelled out in public until now. Why?

LEARY: The sexual impact is, of course, the open but private secret about LSD, which none of us has talked about in the last few years. It's socially dangerous enough to say that LSD helps you find divinity and helps you discover yourself. You're already in trouble when you say that. But then if you announce that the psychedelic experience is basically a *sexual* experience, you're asking to bring the whole middle-aged, middle-class monolith down on your head. At the present time, however, I'm under a thirty-year sentence of imprisonment, which for a forty-five-year-old man is essentially a life term, and in addition, I am under indictment on a second marijuana offense involving a 16-year sentence. Since there is hardly anything more that middle-aged, middle-class authority can do to me—and since the secret is out anyway among the young—I feel I'm free at this moment to say what we've never said before: that sexual ecstasy is the basic reason for the current LSD boom. When Dr. Goddard, the head of the Food and Drug Administration, announced in a Senate hearing that 10 percent of our college students are taking LSD, did you ever wonder why? Sure, they're discovering God and meaning; sure, they're discovering themselves; but did you really think that sex wasn't the fundamental reason for this surging, youthful social boom? You can no more do research on LSD and leave out sexual ecstasy than you can do microscopic research on tissue and leave out cells.

LSD is not an automatic trigger to sexual awakening, however. The first 10 times you take it, you might not be able to have a sexual experience at all, because you're so overwhelmed and delighted—or frightened and confused—by the novelty; the idea of having sex might be irrelevant or incomprehensible at the moment. But it depends upon the setting and the partner. It is almost inevitable, if a man and his mate take LSD together, that their sexual energies will be unimaginably intensified, and unless clumsiness or fright on the part of one or the other blocks it, it will lead to a deeper experience than they ever thought possible.

From the beginning of our research, I have been aware of this tremendous personal power in LSD. You must be very careful to take it only with someone you know really well, because it's almost inevitable that a woman will fall in love with the man who shares her LSD experience. Deep and lasting neurological imprints, profound emotional bonds, can develop as a result of an LSD session—bonds that can last a lifetime. For this reason, I have always been extremely cautious about running sessions with men and women. We always try to have a subject's husband or wife present during his or her first session, so that as these powerful urges develop, they are directed in ways that can be lived out responsibly after the session.

PLAYBOY: Are you preaching psychedelic monogamy?

LEARY: Well, I can't generalize, but one of the great lessons I've learned from LSD is that every man contains the essence of all men and every woman has within her *all* women. I remember a session a few years ago in which, with horror and ecstasy, I opened my eyes and looked into Rosemary's eyes and was pulled into the deep pools of her being floating softly in the center of her mind, experiencing everything that she was experiencing, knowing every thought that she had ever had. As my eyes were riveted to hers, her face began to melt and change. I saw her as a young girl, as a baby, as an old woman with gray hair and seamy, wrinkled face. I saw her as a witch, a madonna, a nagging crone, a radiant queen, a Byzantine virgin, a tired, worldly-wise oriental whore who had seen every sight of life repeated a thousand times. She was *all* women, all *woman,* the essence of female—eyes smiling, quizzically, resignedly, devilishly, always inviting: "See me, hear me, join me, merge with me, keep the dance going." Now the implications of this experience for sex and mating, I think, are obvious. It's because of this, not because of moral restrictions or restraints, that I've been extremely monogamous in my use of LSD over the last six years.

PLAYBOY: When you speak of monogamy, do you mean complete sexual fidelity to one woman?

LEARY: Well, the notion of running around trying to find different mates is a very low-level concept. We are living in a world of expanding population in which there are more and more beautiful young girls coming off the assembly line each month. It's obvious that the sexual criteria of the past are going to be changed, and that what's demanded of creatures with our sensory and cellular repertoire is not just one affair after another with one young body after another, but the exploration of the incredible depths and varieties of your own identity with a single member of the opposite sex. This involves time and commitment to the voyage. . . . There is a certain kind of neurological and cellular fidelity that develops. I have said for many years now that in the future the grounds for divorce would not be that your wife went to bed with another man and bounced around on a mattress for an hour or two, but that your wife had an LSD session with somebody else, because the bonds and the connections that develop are so powerful.

PLAYBOY: It's been reported that when you are in the company of women, quite a lot of them turn on to you. As a matter of fact, a friend of yours told us that you could have two or three different women every night if you wanted to. Is he right?

LEARY: For the most part, during the last six years, I have lived very quietly in our research centers. But on lecture tours and in highly enthusiastic social gatherings, there is no question that a charismatic public figure does generate attraction and stimulate a sexual response.

PLAYBOY: How often do you return this response?

LEARY: Every woman has built into her cells and tissues the longing for a hero, sage-mythic male, to open up and share her own divinity. But casual sexual encounters do not satisfy this deep longing. Any charismatic person who is conscious of his own mythic potency awakens this basic hunger in women and pays reverence to it at the level that is harmonious and appropriate at the time. Compulsive body grabbing, however, is rarely the vehicle of such communication.

PLAYBOY: Do you disapprove of the idea of casual romance—catalyzed by LSD?

LEARY: Well, I'm no one to tell anyone else what to do. But I would say, if you use LSD to make out sexually in the seductive sense, then you'll be a very humiliated and embarrassed person, because it's just not going to work. On LSD, her eyes would be microscopic, and she'd see very plainly what you were up to, coming on with some heavy-handed, moustache-twisting routine. You'd look like a consummate ass, and she'd laugh at you, or you'd look like a monster and she'd scream and go into a paranoid state. Nothing good can happen with LSD if it's used crudely or for power or manipulative purposes.

PLAYBOY: Suppose you met a girl at a party, developed an immediate rapport, and you both decided to share an LSD trip that same night. Could it work under those circumstances?

LEARY: You must remember that in taking LSD with some-

one else, you are voluntarily relinquishing all of your personality defenses and opening yourself up in a very vulnerable
manner. If you and the girl are ready to do this, there would be
an immediate and deep rapport if you took a trip together.
People from the LSD cult would be able to do it upon a brief
meeting, but an inexperienced person would probably find it
extremely confusing, and the people might become quite isolated from each other. They might be whirled into the rapture
or confusion of their own inner workings and forget entirely
that the other person is there.

PLAYBOY: According to some reports, LSD can trigger the
acting out of latent homosexual impulses in ostensibly heterosexual men and women. Is there any truth to that, in your
opinion?

LEARY: On the contrary, the fact is that LSD is a specific *cure*
for homosexuality. It's well known that most sexual perversions
are the result not of biological binds but of freaky, dislocating
childhood experiences of one kind or another. Consequently,
it's not surprising that we've had many cases of long-term
homosexuals who, under LSD, discover that they are not only
genitally but genetically male, that they are basically attracted
to females. The most famous and public of such cases is that of
Allen Ginsberg, who has openly stated that the first time he
turned on to women was during an LSD session several years
ago. But this is only one of many such cases.

PLAYBOY: Has this happened with Lesbians?

LEARY: I was just going to cite such a case. An extremely
attractive girl came down to our training center in Mexico. She
was a Lesbian and she was very active sexually, but all of her
energy was devoted to making it with girls. She was at an LSD
session at one of our cottages and went down to the beach and
saw this young man in a bathing suit and—flash!—for the first
time in her life the cellular electricity was flowing in her body
and it bridged the gap. Her subsequent sexual choices were
almost exclusively members of the opposite sex.

For the same reasons, LSD is also a powerful panacea for
impotence and frigidity, both of which, like homosexuality, are

symbolic screw-ups. The LSD experience puts you in touch with the wisdom of your body, of your nervous system, of your cells, of your organs. And the closer you get to the message of the body, the more obvious it becomes that it's constructed and designed to procreate and keep the life stream going. When you're confronted with this basic cellular fact under LSD, you realize that your impotency, or your frigidity, is caused by neuropsychological hang-ups of fear or shame that make no sense to your cells, that have nothing to do with the biochemical forces inside your body urging you to merge and mate with a member of the opposite sex.

PLAYBOY: Does LSD always work as a sexual cure-all?

LEARY: Certainly not. LSD is no guarantee of *any* specific social or sexual outcome. One man may take LSD and leave wife and family and go off to be a monk on the banks of the Ganges. Another may take LSD and go *back* to his wife. It's a highly individual situation. Highly unpredictable. During LSD sessions, you see, there can come a microscopic perception of your routine social and professional life. You may discover to your horror that you're living a robot existence, that your relationships with your boss, your wife and your family are stereotyped, empty and devoid of meaning. At this point, there might come a desire to renounce this hollow existence, to collect your thoughts, to go away and cloister yourself from the world like a monk while you figure out what kind of a life you want to go back to, if any.

Conversely, we've found that in giving LSD to members of monastic sects, there has been a definite tendency for them to leave the monastic life and to find a mating relationship. Several were men in their late forties who had been monks for 15 or 20 years, but who even at this mature age returned to society, married and made the heterosexual adjustment. It's not coincidental that of all those I've given LSD to, the religious group—more than 200 ministers, priests, divinity students and nuns—has experienced the most intense sexual reaction. And in two religious groups that prize chastity and celibacy, there have been wholesale defections of monks and nuns who left their religious orders to get married after a series of LSD experiences. The LSD session, you see, is an overwhelming awakening of experience; it releases potent, primal energies, and one of these is the sexual impulse, which is the strongest impulse at any level of organic life. For the first time in their lives, perhaps, these people were meeting head on the powerful life forces that they had walled off with ritualized defenses and self-delusions.

PLAYBOY: A great deal of what is said about LSD by its proponents, including you, has been couched in terms of religious mysticism. You spoke earlier, in fact, of discovering "divinity" through LSD. In what way is the LSD experience religious?

LEARY: It depends on what you mean by religion. For almost everyone, the LSD experience is a confrontation with new forms of wisdom and energy that dwarf and humiliate man's mind. This experience of awe and revelation is often described as religious. I consider my work basically religious, because it has as its goal the systematic expansion of consciousness and the discovery of energies within, which men call "divine." From the psychedelic point of view, almost all religions are attempts—sometimes limited temporally or nationally—to discover the inner potential. Well, LSD is Western yoga. The aim of all Eastern religion, like the aim of LSD, is basically to get high: that is, to expand your consciousness and find ecstasy and revelation within.

PLAYBOY: Dr. Gerald Klee, of the National Institute of Mental Health, has written: "Those who say LSD expands consciousness would have the task of defining the terms. By any conventional definition, I don't think it does expand the consciousness." What do you think?

LEARY: Well, he's using the narrow, conventional definition of consciousness that psychiatrists have been taught: that there are two levels of consciousness—sleep and symbolic normal awareness. Anything else is insanity. So by conventional definition, LSD does *not* expand symbolic consciousness; thus, it creates psychosis. In terms of his conventional symbol game, Dr. Klee is right. My contention is that his definition is too narrow, that it comes from a deplorable, primitive and superstitious system of consciousness. My system of consciousness—attested to by the experience of hundreds of thousands of trained voyagers who've taken LSD—defines seven different levels of awareness.

PLAYBOY: What are they?

LEARY: The lowest levels of consciousness are sleep and stupor, which are produced by narcotics, barbiturates and our national stupefacient, alcohol. A third level of consciousness is the conventional wakeful state, in which awareness is hooked to conditioned symbols: flags, dollar signs, job titles, brand names, party affiliations and the like. This is the level that most people, including psychiatrists, regard as reality; they don't know the half of it. The next two levels of awareness, somatic and sensory, would, I think, be of particular interest to *Playboy* readers, because most of them are of the younger generation, which is much more sensual than the puritanical Americans of the older generation. In order to reach the somatic and sensory levels, you have to have something that will turn *off* symbols and open up your billions of sensory cameras to the billions of impulses that are hitting them. The chemical that opens the door to this level has been well known for centuries to cultures that stress delicate, sensitive registration of sensory stimulation: the Arab cultures, the Indian cultures, the Mogul cultures. It is marijuana. There is no question that marijuana is a sensual stimulator—and this explains not only why it's favored by young people but why it arouses fear and panic among the middle-aged, middle-class, whiskey-drinking, bluenosed bureaucrats who run the narcotics agencies. If they only knew what they were missing.

But we must bid a sad farewell to the bodily levels of consciousness and go on to the sixth level, which I call the cellular level. It's well known that the stronger psychedelics such as mescaline and LSD take you *beyond* the senses into a world of cellular awareness. Now the neurological fact of the matter is that every one of your 13 billion brain cells is hooked up to some 25,000 other cells, and everything you know comes from a communication exchange at the nerve endings of your cells. During an LSD session, enormous clusters of these cells are turned on, and consciousness whirls into eerie panoramas for which we have no words or concepts. Here the metaphor that's most accurate is the metaphor of the microscope, which brings into awareness cellular patterns that are invisible to the naked eye. In the same way, LSD brings into awareness the cellular conversations that are inaudible to the normal consciousness and for which we have no adequate symbolic language. You become aware of processes you were never tuned in to before. You feel yourself sinking down into the soft tissue swamp of your own body, slowly drifting down dark red waterways and floating through capillary canals, softly propelled through endless cellular factories, ancient fibrous clockworks—ticking, clicking, chugging, pumping relentlessly. Being swallowed up this way by the tissue industries and the bloody, sinewy carryings-on inside your body can be an appalling experience the first time it happens to you. But it can also be an awesome one—fearful, but full of reverence and wonder.

PLAYBOY: Is there more?

LEARY: Yes, and this level is even more strange and terrifying. This is the *pre*cellular level, which is experienced only under a heavy dosage of LSD. Your nerve cells are aware—as Professor Einstein was aware—that all matter, all structure, is pulsating energy; well, there is a shattering moment in the deep psychedelic session when your body, and the world around you, dissolves into shimmering latticeworks of pulsating white waves, into silent, subcellular worlds of shuttling energy. But this phenomenon is nothing new. It's been reported by mystics and visionaries throughout the last 4,000 years of recorded history as "the white light" or the "dance of energy." Suddenly you realize that everything you thought of as reality or even as life itself—including your body—is just a dance of particles. You find yourself horribly alone in a dead, impersonal world of raw energy feeding on your sense organs. This, of course, is one of the oldest oriental philosophic notions, that nothing exists except in the chemistry of your own consciousness. But when it first really happens to you through the experience of LSD, it can come as a terrorizing, isolating discovery. At this point, the unprepared LSD subject often screams out: "I'm dead!" And he sits there transfigured with fear, afraid to move. For the experienced voyager, however, this revelation can be exalting: You've climbed inside Einstein's formula, penetrated to the ultimate nature of matter, and you're pulsing in harmony with its primal, cosmic beat.

PLAYBOY: Has this happened to you often during a session?

LEARY: It's happened to me about half of the 311 times I've taken LSD. And every time it begins to happen, no matter how much experience you've had, there is that moment of terror—because nobody likes to see the comfortable world of objects and symbols and even cells disintegrate into the ultimate physical design.

PLAYBOY: Do you think there may be a deeper level of consciousness beyond the precellular?

LEARY: I hope so. We know that there are many other levels of energy within and around us, and I hope that within our lifetimes we will have these opened up to us, because the fact is that there is no form of energy on this planet that isn't recorded somewhere in your body. Built within every cell are molecular strands of memory and awareness called the DNA code—the genetic blueprint that has designed and executed the construction of your body. This is an ancient strand of molecules that possesses memories of every previous organism that has contributed to your present existence. In your DNA code you have the genetic history of your father and mother. It goes back, back, back through the generations, through the eons. Your body carries a protein record of everything that's happened to you since the moment you were conceived as a one-cell organism. It's a living history of every form of energy transformation on this planet back to that thunderbolt in the Precambrian mud that spawned the life process over two billion years ago. When LSD subjects report retrogression and reincarnation visions, this is not mysterious or supernatural. It's simply modern biogenetics.

PLAYBOY: Tell us more about these visions.

LEARY: Well, we don't know how these memories are stored, but countless events from early and even intrauterine life are registered in your brain and can be flashed into consciousness during an LSD experience.

PLAYBOY: Do you merely remember them, or do you actually relive them?

LEARY: The experiences that come from LSD are actually relived—in sight, sound, smell, taste and touch—exactly the way they happened before.

PLAYBOY: If it's an experience from very early life, how can you be sure it's a true memory rather than a vivid hallucination?

LEARY: It's possible to check out some of these ancient memories, but for the most part these memory banks, which are built into your protein cellular strands, can never be checked on by external observation. Who can possibly corroborate what your nervous system picked up before your birth, inside your mother? But the obvious fact is that your nervous system was operating while you were still in the uterus. It was receiving and recording units of consciousness. Why, then, is it surprising that at some later date, if you have the chemical key, you can release these memories of the nine perilous and exciting months before you were born?

PLAYBOY: Can these memory visions be made selective? Is it possible to travel back in time at will?

LEARY: Yes, it is. That happens to be the particular project that I've been working on most recently with LSD. I've charted my own family tree and traced it back as far as I can. I've tried to plumb the gene pools from which my ancestors emerged in Ireland and France.

PLAYBOY: With what success?

LEARY: Well, there are certain moments in my evolutionary history that I can reach all the time, but there are certain untidy corners in my racial path that I often get boxed into, and because they are frightening, I freak out and open my eyes and stop it. In many of these sessions, back about 300 years, I often run across a particular French-appearing man with a black moustache, a rather dangerous-looking guy. And there are several highly eccentric recurrent sequences in an Anglo-Saxon country that have notably embarrassed me when I relived them in LSD sessions—goings-on that shocked my twentieth-century person.

PLAYBOY: What sort of goings-on?

LEARY: Moments of propagation—scenes of rough ancestral sexuality in Irish barrooms, in haystacks, in canopied beds, in covered wagons, on beaches, on the moist jungle floor—and moments of crisis in which my forebears escape from fang, from spear, from conspiracy, from tidal wave and avalanche. I've concluded that the imprints most deeply engraved in the neurological memory bank have to do with these moments of life-affirming exultation and exhilaration in the perpetuation and survival of the species.

PLAYBOY: But how can you be sure they ever happened?

LEARY: You can't. They may all be nothing more than luridly melodramatic Saturday serials conjured up by my forebrain. But whatever they are—memory or imagination—it's the most exciting adventure I've ever been involved in.

PLAYBOY: In this connection, according to a spokesman for the student left, many former campus activists who've gone the LSD route are "more concerned with what's happening in their heads than what's happening in the world." Any comment?

LEARY: There's a certain truth in that. The insight of LSD leads you to concern yourself more with internal or spiritual values; you realize that it doesn't make any difference what you do on the outside unless you change the inside. If all the Negroes and left-wing college students in the world had Cadillacs and full control of society, they would still be involved in an anthill social system unless they opened themselves up first.

PLAYBOY: Aren't these young ex-activists among an increasing number of students, writers, artists and musicians whom one critic has called "the psychedelic drop-outs"—LSD users who find themselves divested of motivation, unable to readjust to reality or to resume their roles in society?

LEARY: There *is* an LSD drop-out problem, but it's nothing to worry about. It's something to cheer. The lesson I have learned from over 300 LSD sessions, and which I have been passing on to others, can be stated in 6 syllables: Turn on, tune in, drop out. "Turn on" means to contact the ancient energies and wisdoms that are built into your nervous system. They provide unspeakable pleasure and revelation. "Tune in" means to harness and communicate these new perspectives in a harmonious dance with the external world. "Drop out" means to detach yourself from the tribal game. Current models of social adjustment—mechanized, computerized, socialized, intellectualized, televised, Sanforized—make no sense to the new LSD generation, who see clearly that American society is becoming an air-conditioned anthill. In every generation of human history, thoughtful men have turned on and dropped out of the tribal game and thus stimulated the larger society to lurch ahead. Every historical advance has resulted from the stern pressure of visionary men who have declared their independence from the game: "Sorry, George III, we don't buy your model. We're going to try something new"; "Sorry, Louis XVI, we've got a new idea. Deal us out"; "Sorry, LBJ, it's time to mosey on *beyond* the Great Society."

The reflex reaction of society to the creative drop-out is panic and irritation. If anyone questions the social order, he threatens the whole shaky edifice. The automatic, angry reaction to the creative drop-out is that he will become a parasite on the hardworking, conforming citizen. This is not true. The LSD experience does not lead to passivity and withdrawal; it spurs a driving hunger to communicate in new forms, in better ways, to express a more harmonious message, to live a better life. The LSD cult has already wrought revolutionary changes in American culture. If you were to conduct a poll of the creative young musicians in this country, you'd find that at least 80 percent are using psychedelic drugs in a systematic way. And this new psychedelic style has produced not only a new rhythm in modern music but a new decor for our discotheques, a new form of film making, a new kinetic visual art, a new literature, and has begun to revise our philosophic and psychological thinking.

Remember, it's the college kids who are turning on—the

smartest and most promising of the youngsters. What an exciting prospect: a generation of creative youngsters refusing to march in step, refusing to go to offices, refusing to sign up on the installment plan, refusing to climb aboard the treadmill.

PLAYBOY: What *will* they do?

LEARY: Don't worry. Each one will work out his individual solution. Some will return to the establishment and inject their new ideas. Some will live underground as self-employed artists, artisans and writers. Some are already forming small communities out of the country. Many are starting schools for children and adults who wish to learn the use of their sense organs. Psychedelic businesses are springing up: bookstores, art galleries. Psychedelic industries may involve more manpower in the future than the automobile industry has produced in the last 20 years. In our technological society of the future, the problem will be not to get people to work but to develop graceful, fulfilling ways of living a more serene, beautiful and creative life. Psychedelics will help to point the way.

PLAYBOY: Concerning LSD's influence on creativity, Dr. B. William Murphy, a psychoanalyst for the National Institute of Mental Health, takes the view that there is no evidence "that drugs of any kind increase creative potency. One unfortunate effect is to produce an illusion dangerous to people who are creative, who cease then to be motivated to produce something that is genuinely new. And the illusion is bad in making those who are not creative get the idea that they are." What's your reaction?

LEARY: It's unfortunate that most of the scientific studies on creativity have been done by psychologists who don't have one creative bone in their body. They have studied people who by definition are emphatically uncreative—namely, graduate students. Is it any wonder that all the "scientific" studies of LSD and creativity have shown no creative results? But to answer your question, I must admit that LSD and marijuana do not allow you to walk to the piano and ripple off great fugues. Psychedelic drugs, particularly marijuana, merely enhance the senses. They allow you to see and hear new patterns of energy that suggest new patterns for composition. In this way, they enhance the creative perspective, but the ability to convert your new perspective, however glorious it may be, into a communication form still requires the technical skill of a musician or a painter or a composer.

But if you want to find out whether LSD and marijuana have helped creative people, don't listen to a psychiatrist; don't listen to a government bureaucrat. Find the artist and ask *him*. If you want to find out about creativity, ask the creative person. If you want to know what LSD does and whether it's good or bad, don't listen to a cop; don't listen to messianic fanatics like Timothy Leary. Find some friend who has taken LSD and ask *him*. He's the person to believe because you'll know how likely he is to distort things, and then you'll be able to judge on the basis of his statements what LSD has done for him. Then ask other friends about their experiences. Base your opinion about LSD on a series of such interviews, and you will have collected more hard data than any of the public health officials and police officers who are making daily scare statements to the press these days.

PLAYBOY: Are any of these scare statements true? According to a recent report on narcotics addiction published by the Medical Society of the County of New York, for example, "those with unstable personalities may experience LSD-induced psychoses." Is that true?

LEARY: In over 3,000 people that I have personally observed taking LSD, we've had only 4 cases of prolonged psychoses—a matter of, say, 2 or 3 weeks after the session. All of these had been in a mental hospital before, and they were people who could not commit themselves to any stable relationship. And all of these people had nothing going in their lives. They were drifting or floating, with no home or family or any roots, no stable, ongoing life situation to return to. It's dangerous to take a trip if you have no internal trust and no external place to turn to afterward.

PLAYBOY: The same New York Medical Society report also stated that "normal, well-adjusted persons can undergo an acute psychotic break under the influence of LSD." Is there any truth to that?

LEARY: Everyone, normal or neurotic, experiences some fear and confusion during the high-dose LSD session. The outcome and duration of this confusion depends upon your environment and your traveling companions. That's why it's tremendously important that the LSD session be conducted in a protected place, that the person be prepared and that he have an experienced and understanding guide to support and shield him from intrusion and interruption. When unprepared people take LSD in bad surroundings, and when there's no one present who has the skill and courage to guide them through it, then paranoid episodes are possible.

PLAYBOY: Will you describe them?

LEARY: There are any number of forms a paranoid episode can take. You can find yourself feeling that you've lived most of your life in a universe completely of your own, not really touching and harmonizing with the flow of the people and the energies around you. It seems to you that everyone else, and every other organism in creation, is in beatific communion, and only you are isolated by your egocentricity. Every action around you fits perfectly into this paranoid mosaic. Every glance, every look of boredom, every sound, every smile becomes a confirmation of the fact that everyone knows that you are the only one in the universe that's not swinging lovingly and gracefully with the rest of the cosmic dance. I've experienced this myself.

I've also sat with hundreds of people who have been panicked because they were trapped at the level of cellular reincarnation, where they looked out and saw that their body had scales like a fish or felt that they had turned into an animal. And I've sat with people who were caught on the electronic level, in that eerie, inhuman world of shuttling vibrations. But all these episodes can be dealt with easily by an experienced guide who recognizes where the LSD tripper is caught. He can bring you back down quite simply by holding a candle in front of you, or getting you to concentrate on your breathing, or having you lie down and getting you to feel your body merging with the mattress or the floor. If he understands the map of conscious-ness, it's very easy to bring you back to a more recognizable and less frightening level. With his help, you'll be able to exult in and learn from the experience.

If he's frightened or uncomprehending, however, or if he acts so as to protect his own social interests, your own terror and confusion are naturally increased. If he treats you as a psychotic rather than as one who is seriously groping with basic problems that you should be encouraged to face and work through, you may be forced into a psychotic state. Every case of prolonged LSD psychosis is the fault not of the drug nor of the drug taker but of the people around him who lose their cool and call the cops or the doctors. The lesson here is to fear neither LSD nor your own psychological nature—which is basically okay—but to fear the diagnosing mind of the psychiatrist. Ninety percent of the bad LSD trips are provoked by psychiatric propaganda, which creates an atmosphere of fear rather than of courage and trust. If the psychiatrists had their way, we'd *all* be patients.

PLAYBOY: Speaking of patients, a recent *Time* essay reported that a survey in Los Angeles "showed as many as 200 victims of bad trips in the city's hospitals at one time." Does that sound to you like a realistic figure?

LEARY: I'd like to know who conducted that survey and where they got their figures, because it's contradicted by the known facts. I was recently told by the director of a large Cali-fornia hospital, which handles LSD cases, that most LSD panic subjects are given a tranquilizer and sent home without even being admitted. The same is true at Bellevue and throughout the country.

PLAYBOY: In the same essay, *Time* wrote: "Under the influ-ence of LSD, nonswimmers think they can swim, and others think they can fly. One young man tried to stop a car on Los Angeles' Wilshire Boulevard and was hit and killed. A magazine salesman became convinced that he was the Messiah." Are these cases, and others like them, representative reactions to LSD, in your opinion?

LEARY: I would say that one case in 10,000 is going to flip out and run out into the street and do something bizarre. But these are the cases that get reported in the papers. There are 3,000 Americans who die every year from barbiturates, and it never hits the papers. Thousands more die in car crashes and from lung cancer induced by smoking. That isn't news, either. But one LSD kid rushes out and takes off his clothes in the street and it's headlines in the New York *Daily News.* If one nut who's a member of the narcotics squad from the Los Angeles police force gets drunk and climbs into an airplane and threatens the pilot, that's no reason for grounding all airplanes, calling alcohol illegal, outlawing guns and dissolving the narcotics bureau of the Los Angeles Police Force. So one episode out of 10,000 LSD cases is no reason for any kind of hand wringing and grandmotherly panic.

PLAYBOY: A recent case of this nature involved a young man who contended that he killed his mother-in-law while he was on LSD. Isn't that a cause for concern?

LEARY: Yes—but only because this one episode has led to some psychiatrists and police calling LSD a homicidal drug. Actually, there's no evidence that that unfortunate boy ever took LSD. He was obviously attempting a cop-out when he talked to the police about it afterward.

PLAYBOY: There have also been reports of suicide under the influence of LSD. Does this happen?

LEARY: In 23 years of LSD use, there has been one definite case of suicide during the LSD session. This was a woman in Switzerland who'd been given LSD without her knowledge. She thought she was going crazy and jumped out of the window. But it wasn't that the LSD poisoned her. The unexpected LSD led to such panic and confusion that she killed herself. There have been other rumors about LSD panics leading to suicide, but I am waiting for the scientific evidence. In more than a million LSD cases, there haven't been more than one or two documented cases of homicide or suicide attributable to the LSD experience.

PLAYBOY: Though it hasn't led to any reported deaths, a

number of LSD panics have been attributed to the experience
of many users, in the midst of a session, that they're about to
have a heart attack. Is this a common occurrence?

LEARY: Fairly common. When somebody says to us in an LSD
session, "My heart's going to stop!" we say, "Okay, fine. That's a
new experience, nothing to be afraid of. Let it stop." There is
no physiological change in your heart, but the experience is
that the heart is stopping. On LSD, you see, you may actually
hear the thump of your heartbeat. You become aware of its
pulsing nerves and muscle fibers straining for the next beat.
How can they possibly do this over and over again? If you're
unprepared for it, this can become a terror that it cannot continue. Because of LSD's distension of the time dimension, you
may wait what seems like five hours for the second beat. Then
you wait again, and you wait, and you are aware of the millions
of cells that must be tiring out; they may not have the strength
to beat again. You're afraid that your heart is going to burst.
Then finally—thump! At last! But did it come slower this time?
Is it stopping? You feel the blood throbbing in your heart. You
feel the ventricles opening and closing; there's a hole in your
heart! The blood is flooding your body! You're drowning in
your own blood! "Help! Get me a doctor!" you may shout. If
this kind of episode occurs, of course, all that's necessary to allay
your fears are a few words of understanding and reassurance
from an experienced guide and companion, who should be with
you at all times.

PLAYBOY: Dr. Jonathan Cole, of the National Institute of
Mental Health, has said that psychedelic drugs "can be dangerous. . . . People go into panic states in which they are ready
to jump out of their skins. . . . The benefits are obscure."
What do you say?

LEARY: Based on the evidence that Dr. Cole has had at hand,
he is justified in saying that. Dr. Cole undoubtedly has never
taken LSD himself. He *has* sponsored research that has been
done—indeed, must be done—in mental hospitals, under psychiatric supervision. But this is the worst possible place to take
LSD. Take LSD in a nuthouse and you'll have a nuthouse

experience. These poor patients are usually not even told what drugs they're given; they're not prepared. I consider this psychological rape. So I'm not surprised that the cases Dr. Cole has heard about from his researchers are negative.

But Dr. Cole doesn't listen to the hundreds of thousands of people who have taken LSD under intelligent, aesthetic, carefully planned circumstances and have had their lives changed for the better. He doesn't receive the hundred letters a week that I receive from people who are profoundly grateful to have been dramatically opened up by LSD. He hears only the horror stories. If you talk to a mortician, you'll come to the conclusion that everyone who is of any importance is dead. If you talk to a law-enforcement officer, you'll find that practically everyone is a criminal, actual or potential. And if you talk to a psychiatrist, you'll hear nothing but gloomy lexicons of psychopathology. What Dr. Cole thinks about LSD is irrelevant, because for every case that his federal researchers have studied, there are 5,000 serious-minded, courageous young laymen out in the universities and out in the seminaries and in their own homes and on the beaches who are taking LSD and having fantastically beautiful experiences.

PLAYBOY: Have you allowed or encouraged your children to use marijuana and LSD?

LEARY: Yes. I have no objection to them expanding their consciousness through the use of sacramental substances in accord with their spiritual growth and well-being. At Harvard, in Mexico and here at Millbrook, both of my children have witnessed more psychedelic sessions than any psychiatrist in the country.

PLAYBOY: At most of the psychedelic sessions you've conducted in the course of research, as you've said elsewhere, you and your associates have turned on with your subjects—and not in the laboratory but on beaches, in meadows, living rooms and even Buddhist temples. In the opinion of most authorities, this highly unconventional therapeutic technique is not only impractical but irrational and irresponsible. How do you justify it?

LEARY: This sort of criticism has ruined my reputation in

conventional research circles, but it simply betrays ignorance of the way LSD works. You have to take it with your patient—or at least to have taken it yourself—in order to empathize with and follow him as he goes from one level to another. If the therapist has never taken it, he's sitting there with his sticky molasses Freudian psychiatric chessboard attempting to explain experiences that are far beyond the narrow limits of that particular system.

PLAYBOY: You've also been criticized for being insufficiently selective in the screening of subjects to whom you've administered LSD.

LEARY: We have been willing and eager to run LSD sessions with anyone in any place that made collaborative sense to me and the subject. We've never given LSD to anyone for our own selfish purposes, or for selfish purposes of his own, but if any reasonably stable individual wanted to develop his own consciousness, we turned him on. This ruined our reputation with scientists, of course, but it also made possible a fantastically successful record: 99 percent of the people who took LSD with us had fabulous experiences. None of our subjects flipped out and went to Bellevue; they walked out of the session room with messianic gleams in their eyes.

PLAYBOY: Even if only one percent of your subjects had bad experiences, is it worth the risk?

LEARY: That question can be answered only by the individual. When men set out for Plymouth in a leaky boat to pursue a new spiritual way of life, of course they were taking risks. But the risks of the voyage were less than the risks of remaining in a spiritual plague area, immobilized from the possibility of change by their fears of taking a risk. No government bureau or Big Brother doctor can be allowed to decide who is going to take the risks involved in this twentieth-century voyage of spiritual discovery.

PLAYBOY: Yet restrictive and prohibitive laws against the use of LSD have already been passed in California, Nevada and New Jersey, and several members of Congress have urged federal legislation outlawing its manufacture or possession.

LEARY: Such laws are unrealistic and unconstitutional. Over 15 percent of college students are currently using LSD. Do the hard-arteried politicians and police types really want to put our brightest and most creative youngsters in prison for possession of a colorless, odorless, tasteless, nonaddictive, mind-opening substance? Irrational, senile legislation preventing people from pursuing private, intimate experiences—sexual or spiritual—cannot and will not be obeyed. We are currently planning to appeal any conviction for possession of LSD on constitutional grounds. But the federal government is opposed to laws penalizing possession of LSD because it recognizes the impossibility of enforcement and the unconstitutionality of such statutes. Of course, this ambiguous situation is temporary. In 15 years, the bright kids who are turning on now will be shaping public opinion, writing our novels, running our universities and repealing the hysterical laws that are now being passed.

PLAYBOY: In what way are they hysterical?

LEARY: They're hysterical because the men who are passing them have allowed their ignorance of LSD to escalate into irrationality. Instinctively they put LSD in the same bag with heroin. They think of drug taking as a criminal activity practiced by stuporous escapists and crazed, deranged minds. The daily diatribes of police officials and many legislators to that effect completely ignore the fact that the use of LSD is a white-collar, upper-middle-class, college-educated phenomenon. The LSD user is not a criminal type. He's not an underground character or a junkie. He doesn't seek to hide or to apologize for his activities. But while more and more laws are being passed restricting these activities, more and more people are engaging in them. LSD is being manufactured by people in their own homes and in small laboratories. If this continues, in ten years the LSD group will constitute one of our largest minorities. Then what are the lawmakers going to do?

PLAYBOY: What *should* they do, in your opinion?

LEARY: As they learn more about LSD, I think—I hope—they will recognize that there will have to be special legislation. There *should* be laws about the manufacture of LSD. It is an incredibly powerful drug. It is not a narcotic and not a medical drug; it doesn't cure any illness. It is a new form of *energy*. Just as a new form of legislation had to be developed for radioactive isotopes, so will there need to be something comparable for LSD. And I think some LSD equivalent of the Atomic Energy Commission and some special licensing procedures should be set up to deal with this new class of drugs.

PLAYBOY: What sort of procedures would you recommend?

LEARY: You can't legalize and control manufacture until you've worked out a constructive way of licensing or authorizing possession. There are many individuals who should be provided with a legitimate access to chemicals that expand their minds. If we don't do this, we'll have a free market or a black market. During Prohibition, when alcohol was prohibited, it was suppressed; then you had bathtub gin and bootleg poisons of all sorts. The government received no taxes and the consumer had no guarantee that what he was buying was safe and effective. But if marijuana and LSD were put under some form of licensing where responsible, serious-minded people could purchase these chemicals, then the manufacture could be supervised and the sales could be both regulated and taxed. A healthy and profitable situation would result for all involved.

PLAYBOY: How would a person demonstrate his responsibility and serious-mindedness in applying for a license?

LEARY: The criteria for licensing the use of mild psychedelics like marijuana should be similar to those for the automobile license. The applicant would demonstrate his seriousness by studying manuals, passing written tests and getting a doctor's certificate of psychological and physical soundness. The licensing for use of powerful psychedelic drugs like LSD should be along the lines of the airplane pilot's license: intensive study and preparation, plus very stringent testing for fitness and competence.

PLAYBOY: What criteria would you use for determining fitness and competence?

LEARY: No one has the right to tell anyone else what he should or should not do with this great and last frontier of freedom. I think that anyone who wants to have a psychedelic experience and is willing to prepare for it and to examine his own hang-ups and neurotic tendencies should be allowed to have a crack at it.

PLAYBOY: Have you had the opportunity to present this plan to the Federal Narcotics Bureau?

LEARY: I would be most happy to, but the Narcotics people don't want any sort of objective, equal-play consideration of these issues. When anyone suggests the heretical notion that LSD be made available to young people or even hints, let us say, at the necessity for scientific evaluation of marijuana, he is immediately labeled as a dangerous fanatic and is likely to be investigated. This certainly has been demonstrated by reactions of people asked to contribute to my legal defense fund. There are hundreds who have contributed but who realistically cannot afford to have their names involved in such a case, because they believe public identity may lead to investigatory persecution.

Playboy is among the rare institutions that will tackle an issue of this sort. There is an enormous amount of peripheral harassment. . . . This issue has generated so much hysteria that the normal processes of democratic debate are consistently violated. When several million Americans can't have their voices heard and can't get objective and scientific consideration of their position, I think that the Constitution is in danger.

PLAYBOY: There are some who see the appeal of your conviction in Laredo as a step leading to legalization of marijuana. Do you think that's possible?

LEARY: If I win my case in the higher courts—and my lawyers believe I will—this will have wide implications. It will suggest that future arrests for marijuana must be judged on the merits of the individual case rather than a blanket, arbitrary implementation of irrational and excessive regulation. I consider the marijuana laws to be unjust laws. My 30-year sentence and $30,000 fine simply pointed up in a rather public way the severity and harshness of the current statutes, which are clearly in violation of several amendments to the Constitution.

PLAYBOY: Which amendments?

LEARY: The First Amendment, which guarantees the right of spiritual exploration, and the Fifth Amendment, which guarantees immunity from self-incrimination. The fact that I'm being imprisoned for not paying a tax on a substance that, if I had applied for a license, would have led to my automatic arrest, is clearly self-incrimination. The current marijuana statutes are also in violation of the Eighth Amendment, which forbids cruel and unusual punishments, and of the Ninth Amendment, which guarantees certain personal liberties not specifically enumerated in the other amendments.

PLAYBOY: The implications of your arrest and conviction in Laredo were still being debated when the police raided your establishment here in Millbrook. We've read several different versions of just what took place that night. Will you give us a step-by-step account?

LEARY: Gladly. On Saturday, April 16th, there were present at our center in Millbrook 29 adults and 12 children. Among them were 3 Ph.D. psychologists, 1 M.D. psychiatrist, 3 physicists, 5 journalists on professional assignments and 3 photographers. At 1:30 A.M., all but 3 guests had retired. I was in bed. My son and a friend of his were in the room talking to me about a term paper that my son was writing. We heard a noise outside in the hallway. My son opened the door, slammed it and said, "Wow, Dad, there's about 50 cops out there!" I jumped out of bed and was in the middle of the room when the door burst open and 2 uniformed sheriffs and 2 assistant district attorneys marched in and told me not to move. I was wearing only pajama tops.

One of the sheriff's statements to the press was that the raiding party discovered most of the occupants in the house in a state of semiundress—which sounds pretty lurid until you realize that almost everyone in the house was in bed asleep at the time of the raid. After the initial shock of finding armed and uniformed men in our bedrooms, all of my guests reacted with patience, humor and tolerance to five hours of captivity. The members of the raiding party, on the other hand, were extremely nervous. It's obvious that they had in mind some James

Bond fantasy of invading the oriental headquarters of some sexual SMERSH, and they were extremely jumpy as they went about their search of the entire house. One interesting aspect of the raid was that all of the women present were stripped and searched.

PLAYBOY: Did anyone object?

LEARY: We objected to *everything* that was being done, including the fact that we could not have a lawyer present.

PLAYBOY: What did the police find during the search?

LEARY: After a 5-hour search, they arrested 4 people: a photographer here on a professional assignment, and a Hindu holy man and his wife—all of whom they alleged had marijuana in their possession—and myself. There was no claim that I had any marijuana in my possession or control; the charge involved my being the director of the house.

PLAYBOY: Did they have a warrant?

LEARY: They had a warrant, but we claim it was defective and illegal.

PLAYBOY: In what way?

LEARY: In the Bill of Rights it clearly states that the government cannot just swear out a warrant to go into anyone's house on general suspicion and speculation. Specifically, a search warrant can be issued only on the basis of tangible evidence, usually from an informer, that a specific amount of defined, illegal substance is present at a certain place and time. There was no such probable cause for the raid at Millbrook. Among the "causes" cited was that cars with out-of-state licenses were parked in my driveway, and that girls under the age of sixteen were playing around the yard on a certain day when it was under surveillance.

PLAYBOY: How would that be a cause?

LEARY: How, indeed? Another alleged "cause" for the raid was that I am "a known and admitted trafficker in drugs." Well, none of these espionage reports seem to me—or to my lawyers—to justify the issuance of a no-knock, nighttime warrant that authorized the breaking of windows and doors to obtain entry to a private house.

PLAYBOY: What is the current status of the charges against you?

LEARY: We are now involved in nine pieces of litigation on this raid. The American Civil Liberties Union has entered the case with a supporting brief, and while I can't comment on the technicalities of the litigation, we have a large group of bright young turned-on civil libertarian lawyers walking around with smiles on their faces.

PLAYBOY: Do you mean that your lawyers are on LSD?

LEARY: I don't feel I should comment on that. Let me say, however, that you don't need to *use* anything to be turned on, in the sense that you've tuned in to the world.

PLAYBOY: Dr. Humphrey Osmond of the New Jersey Neuropsychiatric Institute—the man who coined the word "psychedelic"—has described you as "Irish and revolutionary, and to a good degree reckless." He was suggesting that if you had been more careful, you might not have been arrested in Laredo or Millbrook.

LEARY: I plead guilty to the charges of being an Irishman and a revolutionary. But I don't think I'm careless about anything that's important.

PLAYBOY: Wasn't it careless to risk the loss of your freedom by carrying a half ounce of marijuana into Mexico?

LEARY: Well, that's like saying, wouldn't it be careless for a Christian to carry the Bible to Russia? I just can't be bothered with paranoias about wiretapping, surveillance and police traps. It's been well known for several years that I'm using psychedelic drugs in my own home and in my own center for the use of myself and my own family. So at any time the government wanted to make an issue of this, it certainly could. But I can't live my life in secrecy or panic paranoia. I've never bothered to take a lot of elementary precautions, for example, about my phone being bugged or my actions being under surveillance— both of which the police admit. I would say that if there was carelessness in Laredo, it was carelessness on the part of the government officials in provoking a case that has already changed public attitudes and will inevitably change the law on the possession and use of marijuana by thoughtful adults in this country. The Narcotics Bureau is in trouble. I'm not.

PLAYBOY: But suppose all appeals fail and you do go to prison. What will happen to your children and to your work?

LEARY: My children will continue to grow—externally and internally—and they and all of my friends and colleagues will continue to communicate what they've learned to a world that certainly needs such lessons. As to where and how they will live, I can't predict.

PLAYBOY: Have you made any provision for their financial support?

LEARY: At the present time I'm $40,000 in debt for legal expenses, and I have made no provisions for eating lunch tomorrow. But we'll cross that bridge when we come to it.

PLAYBOY: Do you dread the prospect of imprisonment?

LEARY: Well, I belong to one of the oldest trade unions in human civilization—the alchemists of the mind, the scholars of consciousness. The threat of imprisonment is the number-one occupational hazard of my profession. Of the great men of the past whom I hold up as models, almost every one of them has been either imprisoned or threatened with imprisonment for their spiritual beliefs: Gandhi, Jesus, Socrates, Lao-tse. I have absolutely no fear of imprisonment. First of all, I've taken LSD over 40 times in a maximum-security prison as part of a convict rehabilitation project we did in Boston, so I know that the only real prisons are *internal*. Secondly, a man who feels no guilt about his behavior has no fear of imprisonment; I have not one shred of guilt about anything I've done in the last 6 years. I've made hundreds of mistakes, but I've never once violated my own ethical or moral values. I'm the freest man in America today. If you're free in mind and heart, you're not in trouble. I think that the people who are trying to put other people in jail and to control basic evolutionary energies like sex and psychedelic chemicals are in trouble, because they're swimming upstream against the two-billion-year tide of cellular evolution.

PLAYBOY: What would you say is the most important lesson you've learned from your personal use of LSD?

LEARY: First and last, the understanding that basic to the life impulse is the question, should we go *on* with life? This is the only real issue, when you come down to it, in the evolutionary cosmic sense: whether to make it with a member of the opposite sex and keep it going—or not to. At the deepest level of consciousness, this question comes up over and over again. I've struggled with it in scores of LSD sessions. How did we get here and into this mess? How do we get out? There are two ways out of the basic philosophic isolation of man: You can ball your way out—by having children, which is immortality of a sort. Or you can step off the wheel. Buddhism, the most powerful psychology that man has ever developed, says essentially that. My choice, however, is to keep the life game going. I'm Hindu, not Buddhist.

Beyond this affirmation of my own life, I've learned to confine my attention to the philosophic questions that hit on the really shrieking, crucial issues: Who wrote the cosmic script? What does the DNA code expect of me? Is the big genetic-code show live or on tape? Who is the sponsor? Are we completely trapped inside our nervous systems, or can we make *real* contact with anyone else out there? I intend to spend the rest of my life, with psychedelic help, searching for the answers to these questions—and encouraging others to do the same.

PLAYBOY: What role do you think psychedelics will play in the everyday life of the future?

LEARY: A starring role. LSD is only the first of many new chemicals that will exhilarate learning, expand consciousness and enhance memory in years to come. These chemicals will inevitably revolutionize our procedures of education, child rearing and social behavior. Within one generation these chemical keys to the nervous system will be used as regular tools of learning. You will be asking your children, when they come home from school, not "What book are you reading?" but "Which molecules are you using to open up new Libraries of Congress inside your nervous system?" There's no doubt that chemicals will be the central method of education in the future. The reason for this, of course, is that the nervous system, and learning and memory itself, is a chemical process. A society in which a large percentage of the population changes consciousness regularly and harmoniously with psychedelic drugs will bring about a very different way of life.

PLAYBOY: Will there be a day, as some science fiction writers predict, when people will be taking trips, rather than drinks, at psychedelic cocktail parties?

LEARY: It's happening already. In this country, there are already functions at which LSD may be served. I was at a large dance recently where two-thirds of the guests were on LSD. And during a scholarly LSD conference in San Francisco a few months ago, I went along with 400 people on a picnic at which almost everyone turned on with LSD. It was very serene. They were like a herd of deer in the forest.

In years to come, it will be possible to have a lunch-hour psychedelic session; in a limited way, that can be done now with DMT, which has a very fast action, lasting perhaps a half hour. It may be that there will also be large reservations of maybe 30 or 40 square miles, where people will go to have LSD sessions in tranquil privacy.

PLAYBOY: Will the psychedelic experience become universal? Will everyone be turned on?

LEARY: Well, not all the time. There will always be some functions that require a narrow form of consciousness. You don't want your airplane pilot flying higher than the plane and having Buddhist revelations in the cockpit. Just as you don't play golf on Times Square, you won't want to take LSD where narrow, symbol-manipulating attention is required. In a sophisticated way, you'll attune the desired level of consciousness to the particular surrounding that will feed and nourish you.

No one will commit his life to any single level of consciousness. Sensible use of the nervous system would suggest that a quarter of our time will be spent in symbolic activities—producing and communicating in conventional, tribal ways. But the fully conscious life schedule will also allow considerable time—perhaps an hour or two a day—devoted to the yoga of the senses, to the enhancement of sensual ecstasies through marijuana and hashish, and one day a week to completely moving outside the sensory and symbolic dimensions into the transcendental realms that are open to you through LSD. This is not science fiction fantasy. I have lived most of the last six years—until the recent unpleasantness—doing exactly that: taking LSD once a week and smoking marijuana once a day.

PLAYBOY: How will this psychedelic regimen enrich human life?

LEARY: It will enable each person to realize that he is not a game-playing robot put on this planet to be given a Social Security number and to be spun on the assembly line of school, college, career, insurance, funeral, good-bye. Through LSD, each human being will be taught to understand that the entire history of evolution is recorded inside his body; the challenge of the complete human life will be for each person to recapitulate and experientially explore every aspect and vicissitude of this ancient and majestic wilderness. Each person will become his own Buddha, his own Einstein, his own Galileo. Instead of relying on canned, static, dead knowledge passed on from other symbol producers, he will be using his span of 80 or so years on this planet to live out every possibility of the human, prehuman and even subhuman adventure. As more respect and time are diverted to these explorations, he will be less hung up on trivial, external pastimes. And this may be the natural solution to the problem of leisure. When all of the heavy work and mental drudgery is taken over by machines, what are we going to do with ourselves—build even bigger machines? The obvious and only answer to this peculiar dilemma is that man is going to have to explore the infinity of inner space, to discover the terror and adventure and ecstasy that lie within us all.

8

Drop Out or Cop Out

It's always been that way, and it will always be that way. There are two societies, two symbiotic cultures uneasily sharing this planet, two intertwined human structures, mirror-imaged like root and branch. The overground and the underground. The drop-outs and the cop-outs.

There is the visible establishment—officious, federal, rational, organized, uniformed, at times grim, at times smug in its apparent control of external power—metal, machines, weapons. The cop-outs. The cops.

And there is the drop-out underground—loose, sloppy, foolish, tenacious, private, at times joyous, at times paranoid. Protected by its camouflage, conspiratorial laughter, the knowing glance, the facade of poverty, long hair, out-of-fashion dress, the covert subtle gesture, the double meaning, sustained by its access to inner power—touch, taste, sensual connections, laughter, smell, moist contact, ecstasy.

The external power structure is forever rent by struggles for material control, national rivalries, economic competition, political conflicts, ideologies of might. The boring battles of generals and politicians. The CIA versus the FBI.

The underground society is also divided on the basis of somatic, domestic, sensory, erotic, ritual, chemical preferences. The battles of clans and cults. Of magicians and saints.

This ancient duality has reached an evolutionary crisis point today. To see what's happening (and it's never reported in the papers), you have to be aware of this overground-underground ballet. But to see it, you have to be underground. The overground establishment today just can't see what's happening, can't accept the dedicated, enduring, inevitable existence of the underground. LBJ has no logical, rational categories to deal with the apolitical smile. The soft chuckle which comes from neither the left nor the right but some center within.

In earlier, wiser times this struggle was clearly recognized as the essential battle between God and the devil, in which the devil (who is always he who controls the external power) systematically switches the labels (for obvious tactical reasons) and calls the static, regulated, dry, grim, humorless, destructive antilife GOOD and the free, ecstatic, sensual, moist, funny, joyous BAD. This doesn't fool the turned-on undergrounders, who are hip to the fact that God is a singing, swinging energy process who likes to laugh and make love and burrow, murmuring, underground.

The underground is always aware of the existence and reflex responses of the overground. Survival in the underground depends on your ability to anticipate the movements of external power. It's always been a capital crime to laugh, make love, and turn on barefoot in front of whitey's house, and these are the endemic, chronic crimes of the giggling young, the colored, the artists and the visionaries.

The structure of the overground is always obsessively and specifically organized. Read the rule books and directories. Today the whole freaky social structure is listed alphabetically in the yellow pages of the phone book. Read the section solemnly listing the local offices of the U.S. government, for example. Isn't that weird?

The structure of the underground is equally explicit and obvious to those in the know, but this knowledge is experiential, whispered, word-of-mouth, friend to friend and rarely written down. Can you write down a good joke? The telephone directory has no listing for the soft essences, the chemical secretions of life, love goddesses, alchemists, ecstasy drugs, astrologers, religious experiences, prophetic visions, fun, laughter, wry humor, the warm hand that slips under your pretenses and

touches you in exactly the right place. Where are these classi-
fied?

The underground is always composed of the "outs," those
who are alienated from the establishment power centers—in-
voluntarily by deprivation or voluntarily by aesthetic-religious
choice. The young, the poor, the racially rejected, the articu-
lately sensitive, the spiritually turned on are curious, sensual,
ecstatic, erotic, shameless, free, mischievous, rebellious, intuitive, humorous, playful, spiritual. Adults, the middle class, the
cops, the government men, the educators, those people listed in
the yellow pages, are not. No funny business here; this is
serious.

In the past the polar tension between the two societies was
balanced by the slow ebb-and-flow tide of history. Underground
pressure builds up gradually over decades. An ecstatic upheaval
from below—Christ, Buddha, Mohammed—then slowly a new
hierarchy emerges. The glue which held the creaky network of
society together in the past was the biological fact of matura-
tion. Social movements come and go, but the kids grew up to be
adults like their parents. Underground kids became underground adults, gypsies, Jews, hustlers, and artists. Middle-class
kids become middle-class adults.

What is new and fascinating about the current upheaval is
this incredible fact: *the kids today are different.* They won't
grow up like Mom and Dad. This is not a sociological trend. It's
an evolutionary lurch. The generation gap is a species mutation. Electronics and psychedelics have shattered the sequence
of orderly linear identification, the automatic imitation that
provides racial and social continuity. The kids today just won't
grow up to be like their parents. They are pulsating television
grids. They move consciousness around by switching channel
knobs. Tune in. Tune out. Flick on. Correct image focus.
Adjust brightness.

Technology moves energy patterns at the speed of light, and
psychochemicals accelerate and switch consciousness in exact
proportions to nuclear power and electric circuitry. Your head is
the cosmic TV show, baby. Alcohol turns off the brightness,

methadrine jiggles and speeds up the image, LSD flips on 87 channels at once, pot adds color, meditation, mantras, prayer, mudras sharpen the focus. It's your head, baby, and it's 2 billion years old, and it's got every control switch that GE and IBM ever thought of and a million more, and it's hooked up in direct connection to Central Broadcasting Station WDNA, and you had better learn to treasure it NOW, because it's planned by the Great Cartel Monopoly Benevolent Corporation, blueprint designer for planned obsolescence every 70 years, and there's no rewind and/or instant replay, baby, so turn on, tune in, drop out NOW!

Consider (as case history illustration) what happened to me yesterday. During the afternoon, voices hurtled at the speed of light up to the third floor at Millbrook from a West German TV producer, from a Japanese TV producer, asking to film the psychedelic scene at Millbrook. We had a dozen long-distance phone calls from people who tuned in last week to the nation-wide program televised at Millbrook. An LSD baby was born to a couple living on the second floor—Negro mother, white father. At moonrise a new tepee, lined for winter living, was inaugurated at the camp of the League for Spiritual Discovery . . . fire crackling . . . scent of incense, pine branches, marijuana . . . 15 high people holding hands in a circle and chanting . . . the play of shadows on the white cone wall.

Before midnight a fifteen-year-old girl on an acid trip in Seattle phoned, requesting a copy of the league manual *How to Start Your Own Religion*. After midnight a college kid from Wisconsin phoned requesting help on a bad trip. At 3 A.M. my eighteen-year-old son Jack phoned from San Francisco. He had taken 1,000 gamma of LSD along with 1,500 other kids at a psychedelic   ballroom . . .   Owsley's   free   sacrament . . . psychedelic lights . . . acid rock 'n' roll. He stated quietly that he was illuminated. None of the parents' manuals tell you what to say when your kid announces he has done the Buddha bit, attained satori. Our sons aren't supposed to become Christ or Lao-tse, are they?

I said, "You're illuminated. Now what?"

Without a second's hesitation, he replied, "Now I illuminate."
Wow! What manual is *he* reading? He had seen everything.
How it all fitted together. All is one. He had been given $17,000
by a teen-age love commune in L.A. to buy acid in San Francisco. Under LSD he had pulled a thousand-dollar bill out of his
pocket and meditated and then burned it. The parents' magazines don't tell you what to say when your son tells you that he's
burned a thousand-dollar bill because money is a paper illusion.

Turn on, tune in, drop out, said Dr. Timothy Leary to the
younger generation. Did I really say that?

Now I am standing, shivering, talking into the hall phone at
three o'clock in the morning, holding the psychedelic prayer
book I wrote in my hand, but it's useless because this son of
mine with dilated pupils is 3,000 miles beyond me and is far
wiser than any bible ever written by old men, read and recited
by the sleepy, shivering, harassed father of two teen-age kids
who have blown their minds with acid and talk quietly about
Nirvana and illusion and the mind trip and the boring, repetitious hypocrisy of adult games. ("Daddy, please don't make
me go back to the tired old game," said my daughter Susan after
the hashish party in Hollywood.) I am the bewildered father of
two unprepared kids who have experienced more than Buddha
and Einstein and are floating with their generation out beyond
my comprehension, and I may well be one of the wisest men
ever born before 1945.

Listen, when I was a forty-year-old smart-aleck atheist Harvard professor and renowned research psychologist, illumination to me meant electric lighting, and consciousness was just
the opposite of what poor Freud talked about. And I've taken
LSD as much as and studied it more than anyone around, and
I'm still left behind, carrying on my shivering shoulders at three
o'clock in the morning the grief and bewilderment of every
parent whose teen-age children are mutating through acid
(lysergic and nucleic) up to a higher level of existence. I can't
give my beautiful, wise, turned-on son any logical reason why
he shouldn't burn a thousand-dollar bill. And if you think you

can, fellow parents, you just don't understand the problem which the Buddha saw and the DNA codes and which your kids are facing in psychedelic-electronic 1968.

Then I talked to the young man from L.A. whose thousand-dollar bill had been burned.

"How is Jack?"

"He's beautiful!"

I said, "My son is far out?" Pause.

"No. He's a Taoist kid. He's one with the flow. You worry him with your worries. Trust him. He loves you." The young man didn't even mention the loss of the money, and when I asked him about it he said, "Well I've always wanted to burn a thousand-dollar bill. Hasn't everybody?" And this from a twenty-two-year-old who lives with his wife and two kids in a small house on $200 a month. I had trouble going back to sleep.

You see, don't you, that you learn nothing about the psychedelic underground and the electronic generation from the establishment press? *Hippy* is an establishment label for a profound, invisible, underground, evolutionary process. For every visible hippy, barefoot, beflowered, beaded, there are a thousand invisible members of the turned-on underground. Persons whose lives are tuned in to their inner vision, who are dropping out of the TV comedy of American life.

Fellow parents, if you have kids between the ages of eleven and twenty-five, chances are you've got the underground working in your own home. "What!" you say. "Horrors! One of our kids a secret hippy? What shall we do? Phone a psychiatrist? Read them the riot act? Call the police?" No. This time, let's try an experiment in listening. Let's initiate an intergeneration probe of peace and trust. Find the member of the underground nearest you—your own child, or your niece, or the boy next door—and consider him for an hour or two as a friendly ambassador sent to you from the world of the future. Listen to him.

Another way is to tune into the communication channels that carry the underground message. Read their newspapers. Every city in the country has its underground paper serving its young readers with the news they want and advertising the commodities they want in the language they understand. Read the *East Village Other*, the *Oracle* of San Francisco or the *Oracle* of Los Angeles, or read any college newspaper that is relatively free of faculty control. You'll be amazed at the consistency and sophistication of the new philosophy.

Listen to their music. The rock 'n' roll bands are the philosopher-poets of the new religion. Their beat is the pulse of the future. The message from Liverpool is the Newest Testament, chanted by four Evangelists—saints John, Paul, George and Ringo. Pure Vedanta, divine revelation, gentle, tender irony at the insanities of war and politics, sorrowful lament for the bourgeois loneliness, delicate hymns of glory to God. And the humor, the sharp, sincere satire of the "put-on," the mild mocking of the pompous, even of one's own inevitable pomposity, even of the ridiculousness of teen-age rock stars becoming holy men, and that's what they really are.

The "put-on," the soft-sell, the double-meaning, easy, relaxed, laughing flow with the Tao stream of life—that's what makes it hard to understand these kids. Our older generation has been enslaved by a heavy, melodramatic view of life. Pitiful Shakespeare! All those grim, suffering, ham-actor heroes sweating out the failure of ambition, the torments of jealousy, the agony of wounded pride, the passions of unrequited love. The Western world has been on a bad trip, a 400-year bummer. War heroics. Guilt. Puritan ethics, grim, serious, selfish, striving. Remember, Mom and Dad, the songs of our youth? The blues. The Stratford-on-Avon masochistic ragtime laments of Tin Pan Alley? Well, that's all over now, Daddy and Mamma Blue. The atom bomb and the electronic flash and the ecstasy drugs have held up a million mocking mirrors to that struggling, bloody, self-pitying, self-indulgent, noble, lonely, martyred stage-TV hero who is you, Mr. and Mrs. America, and that's how your turned-on kids see you and why they sorrow for you and wait to turn you on.

But to learn the lesson from your kids, you've got to groove with their electronic-fluid timeless point of view, which is both the newest and the oldest human philosophy, and accept their up-revision of Shakespeare in which Juliet's sleeping potion becomes a turn-on sacramental love elixir and Romeo took it with her in the tomb and they laughed in ecstatic revelation and pity at that old posturing Montague-Capulet hang-up, and they split together from Verona and opened a lute shop in Rome and stayed high forever after. And then Lady Bird Macbeth built a fire and lit a candle and some incense and put a tender chant on the stereo and rolled a joint of Scotch Broom, and she and Macbeth sat looking into the dancing flame and got soft and high and saw how foolish it was to struggle for the throne and dissolved into love for each other and for their rivals and prayed for them.

Above all, to get the message of the future, sit down with a youngster and relax and tune in to the new theme. You'll be shy and awkward. Your kid may be, too. That's natural. But stay with it and keep serene. Maybe your dialogue will start indirectly by listening together. The best way for any parent to dissolve fear and develop trust in the youngsters is to get the Beatles' "Sergeant Pepper" album or the Rolling Stones' "Satanic Majesties" and take it humbly to a kid and say, "I've heard that there's an important message in this record, but I need it explained to me. Will you talk to me about the Stones and Beatles?" And then get very comfortable and close your eyes and listen to the sermon from Liverpool (it could just as well be Donovan or Dylan or the Jefferson Airplane) and learn that it's the oldest message of love and peace and laughter, and trust in God and don't worry, trust in the future, and don't fight; and trust in your kids, and don't worry because it's all beautiful and right.

9

Hormonal Politics: The Menopausal
Left-Right and the Seed Center

The political spectrum which has colored social attitudes for the past 300 years has decreasing relevance today and by 1980 will have no political meaning.

Left-Right. Liberal-Conservative. Radical-Reactionary. Communist-Capitalist. Democratic-Republican. Whig-Tory. Labor-Management. White-Colored. Brooklyn Dodgers. Twenty-three skidoo.

The crucial variable in today's political equation is age. The basic areas which now divide men are hormonal. The key question to ask a candidate for office—or indeed, any person seeking to influence public opinion—has nothing to do with Vietnam or Marx or John Birch. The issue which determines who will be elected, who will be listened to, is: How much time did you spend making love last week?

Political experts puzzle over the results of recent elections, seeking in vain to find the left-right trend. But one single and simple clue will account, in almost every case, for the surprises and shifts in voting. Age. Can you think of an election return in the last two years which found a potent, seed-carrying candidate defeated by an oldster?

The Kennedy strategy board understands this secret. So do Lindsay and Rockefeller.

War? Peace? Taxes? Race? Nope. Wrinkles.

The Republican party is making a comeback? Nope. They

have been out. Paunchy, jowled Democrats are getting old in office. Outs tend to run younger candidates.

But the Republicans have failed to capitalize completely on this relentless biological advantage because candidate choice is still determined by the most senile members of the Grand Old (sic) Party. Does anyone doubt that young, virile, baby-begetting Rockefeller could have won in 1960 and then in 1964 if the GOP had run him? Does anyone doubt that the Republicans would win in 1968 if they nominated Percy or Lindsay or even new-father Rocky?

This power of hormones in the body politic will steadily increase in the next decade until it becomes the only issue in the 1970's. The current revolution is not economic or religious; it is biological.

Human beings born after the year 1943 belong to a different species from their progenitors. Three new energies, exactly symmetrical and complementary—atomics, electronics, and psychedelics—have produced an evolutionary mutation. The release of atomic energy placed the mysterious basic power of the universe in man's hands. The frailty of the visible. The power of the invisible. Electronic impulses link the globe in an instantaneous communication network. The circuited unity of man. Psychedelic drugs release internal energy and speed consciousness in the same exponential proportions as nuclear and electronic space-time expansions.

Our children were born and have developed in a civilization as far removed from that of their parents as Des Moines, Iowa, is from ancient Carthage. How few parents realized when they quieted their noisy kids by banishing them to the TV room that they were turning on the little ones to a mind-blowing electronic experience. Kiddies flicking the TV knobs. Switch on the news . . . LBJ talking . . . hard sell . . . switch him off . . . Channel 9 . . . cereal commercial, hard sell . . . switch it off . . . Channel 3 . . . Superboy . . . A-OK. Movement. Change. Flashing images. Simultaneity. Multiple choice. And always the hard sell, the come-on promise, and the kids watching warily, catching on to LBJ's pitch and the Corn Flakes pitch, the disillusioning insight through the game facade to the inner essence. The inevitable development of the cool psychology. The hip one who deals with the continual inundation of shifting images, multiplicity of channels, the bending of space-time . . . Apollo rockets . . . DNA . . . overpopulation . . . the ambiguity of good-evil, rich-poor, strong-weak. . . . The old movies replayed . . . endless reminders of the transience of custom and moral . . . did Dad and Mom really dress like that and dance like Fred Astaire and believe those pompous, bigoted, red-faced idiot politicians? The old movies, embarrassingly rerunning time backward . . . humiliating celluloid records of parental capers . . . reincarnation history best left unstudied if you want to preserve naïveté and enthusiasm for the social game and really cheer and cheat and struggle for liberty and Notre Dame and the boys on the battlefront fighting the Kaiser.

Spin faster and faster . . . flip on . . . switch over . . . turn on . . . compress time . . . this is CBC in Saigon . . . space out . . . tune in . . . focus . . . change channels . . . adjust brilliance . . . stroboscopic on-off . . . reality is a flickering grid of electronic images . . . narrow beam . . . stereophonic . . . sonic boom . . . freak out . . . put on . . . make out . . . turn on . . . drop out . . . now-then . . . here-infinity. Wow! The electronic-atomic age is an IBM psychedelic trip kaleidoscopic rocket blast multiphonic and there is no escape and no cop-out, and at age thirteen you are confronted with the choice which the slow linear game of the past allowed you to avoid—robot or Buddha, grin and groove with it or you freeze like the smile on Shirley Temple's face on that late-night flick.

Mao and Ho and Grand Charles and LBJ and Nasser are old mannikin figures from a pre-1914 world which is over. Ta-ta. Good-bye now. A shadowy, dusty, jerky black and white newsreel where men strutted and killed for patriotic virtue, manifest destiny, abstract values, national prestige, revolted against the wicked and conquered the devil enemy who believed in czarism, Communism, Fascism, Hooverism, Catholicism, and all the old, dated chess moves. Mao and LBJ are blood-nerve brothers, twins of the same steel bosom; they think alike. Their world view is basically the same. Like intertwined quarreling lovers, they are both committed to the same marriage—capitalism-Communism. Both drank oil from the same maternal spigot. All the statesmen in the world have more in common with each other than with their own grandchildren. Ho loves Reagan; they share the same game consciousness, and they both avoid the bright, far-seeing eyes of their turned-on teen-agers. De Gaulle waltzes with Prime Minister Wilson, and they both turn off rock 'n' roll.

I remember the phone ringing at Millbrook and a voice with a Russian accent, strange to me but full of love and confidence in my love. "Hello, Tim? This is Andrey. Andrey Voznesensky. We have never met but we are old friends. We have much in common. When can we talk? They are giving me trouble, too."

And I remember the story of Allen Ginsberg being elected the King of the Carnival in Prague and riding in the float cheered by a hundred thousand Czech students while the old World War II Gestapo-style secret police watched and waited to bust Allen alone on the streets at midnight and deport him.

To a large segment, perhaps a majority, of our youth the social reality of the United States makes little sense. They are tuned to a different electronic channel. The reality of a middle-aged American is a fabrication of mass media. TV, newspapers, magazines determine what Mom and Dad believe, like, dislike, desire, value. CBS-UPI-AP-Luce—a million-mouthed monster blindly feeding on its own public-opinion-poll estimates of its own desires. Romney down. Reagan up. Filter cigarettes up. American Motors down. This social reality defined by electronic feedback is a completely artificial closed circuit—a consensual paranoia fabricating its own illusions. The struggle of images.

Romney and Reagan may fascinate middle-aged reporters who write for middle-aged editors in papers supported by middle-aged advertisers and purchased by middle-aged readers—all of whom convince each other that there is something real about the game of Romney and Reagan. But the majority of youth under twenty-five don't read these papers. To them the ridiculous sequence of posture, bluff, deceit, bluster we force upon Romneys and Reagans is as dimly remote and insane as the thrashings of Mao and anti-Mao forces far away in China.

Who cares which impotent, tired old man grabs the power? Johnson? Kosygin? What's the difference? To a growing number of youngsters in America and Russia the political games of the menopausal are ridiculous and immoral. American and Russian editorial writers, equally middle-aged, denounce youth for hooliganism and disrespect for the law. Exactly. The hip youngsters on either side of the Iron Curtain feel amused contempt for police, politicians, educators, generals who struggle to maintain by force a preelectronic, prepsychedelic social ethic of war, worry, competition, threat and fear.

The American youngster is beginning to catch on to the frightening fact (already known by the veterans of the underground, the Negroes, the free artists, the delinquent poor, and the kids of Cuba and Russia) that the affluence and bribery of things and the carnival of televised athletic and political spectacles are the come-on for grim monolithic mind-copping social machines, and for those rebels who spurn the seductive bribe there awaits, on either side of the Iron Curtain, the gun and steel to coerce those who will not conform.

The American youngster who chooses not to buy the system is confronted with a consciousness-control tyranny classically Soviet in its disregard for his individuality. Compulsory education. Can you really believe this phrase, *compulsory education?* This means that if you don't go to the state brainwashing institutes built by the aging, you and your parents are arrested by policemen who carry guns.

Compulsory draft. If you don't want to kill to support the frightened policies of belligerent politicians (hawks, they are called) , you'll go behind steel bars.

Compulsory inhibition of individual freedom to dress and move. The teen-age curfew. Armed police arrest kids for being in the street even with parents' permission. My son Jack was

arrested and jailed along with 50 other youngsters for walking
along Haight Street in San Francisco. I phoned the juvenile
prison.

"Why are you holding my son?"

"He's a suspected runaway."

"He was there with my permission. Now will you release
him?"

"No. The law says he must be held until his parent picks him
up."

"But I'm in New York."

"Sorry, that's the law."

"You mean he has no civil rights in California? They can be
held for no crime?"

"That's right. Until they're eighteen they have no civil
rights."

"And after eighteen you'll draft them, right?"

Remember the photographs in your paper last September of
the high school principal on his hands and knees measuring the
length on the little girl's mini-skirt? And the compulsory cutting of hair?

The average Mom and Dad, sitting gently in front of the
television set, are unaware of the complex guerrilla skirmishes
raging in the streets outside the door between the kids and the
menopausal society. The reflex instinct of distrust and suspicion
of the establishment, the underground—Negroes, Mexicans,
artists, Puerto Ricans, hippies, kids.

The youngsters see it. Skillful and experienced at handling
the media and psychedelic drugs (on which they were nursed),
they know how to react. Take, for example, the classic case of
the Monkees.

Hollywood executives decide to invent and market an American version of the Beatles—the early, preprophetic, cute, yeh-
yeh Beatles. Got it? They audition a hallful of candidates and
type-cast four cute kids. Hire some songwriters. Wire up the
Hooper-rating computer. What do the screaming teeny-boppers
want? Crank out the product and promote it. Feed the great
consumer monster what it thinks it wants, plastic, syrupy, tasty,

marshmallow-filled, chocolate-coated, Saran-wrapped, and sell it. No controversy, no protest. No thinking strange, unique thoughts. No offending Mom and Dad and the advertisers. Make it silly, sun-tanned, grinning ABC-TV.

And what happened? The same thing that happened to the Beatles. The four young Monkees weren't fooled for a moment. They went along with the system but didn't buy it. Like all the beautiful young sons of the new age—Peter Fonda and Robert Walker and young John Barrymore and young Steinbeck and the wise young Hitchcocks—the Monkees use the new energies to sing the new songs and pass on the new message.

The Monkees' television show, for example. Oh, you thought that was silly teen-age entertainment? Don't be fooled. While it lasted, it was a classic Sufi put-on. An early-Christian electronic satire. A mystic-magic show. A jolly Buddha laugh at hypocrisy. At early evening kiddie-time on Monday the Monkees would rush through a parody drama, burlesquing the very shows that glue Mom and Dad to the set during prime time. Spoofing the movies and the violence and the down-heavy-conflict-emotion themes that fascinate the middle-aged.

And woven into the fast-moving psychedelic stream of action were the prophetic, holy, challenging words. Mickey was rapping quickly, dropping literary names, making scholarly references; then the sudden psychedelic switch of the reality channel. He looked straight at the camera, right into your living room, and up-leveled the comedy by saying: "Pretty good talking for a long-haired weirdo, huh, Mr. and Mrs. America?" And then— zap. Flash. Back to the innocuous comedy.

Or, in a spy drama, Mickey warned Peter: "Why, this involves the responsibility for blowing up the entire world!"

Peter, confidentially: "I'll take that responsibility!"

And Mickey, with a glance at the camera, said, "Wow! With a little more ego he'll be ready to run for President."

Why, it all happened so fast, LBJ, you didn't ever see it. Suddenly a whole generation disappeared right from view. Flick. They're gone! They won't vote and they won't listen to the good old promises and threats, and they won't answer

Gallup polls, and they just smile when we arrest them, and they won't be clean-cut, hard-working, sincere, frightened, ambitious boys like Khrushchev and I were. Hey! Where did they go? Flick. Hey, McNamara, fix this set! Ban LSD! Adjust the focus back, call a joint meeting of Congress. McNamara, dammit, boy, fix this set. All I get are flickering, dancing flower swirls of color, and shut off that loud rock 'n' roll beat. McNamara! Westmoreland! Dammit, fix this set! All I hear is the steady drumming beat and laughter, and it's getting softer and it's fading away in the distance. Hey, wait a minute! Come back! Hey, where did they all go?

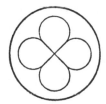

SEAL OF THE LEAGUE

10

*Poet of the Interior Journey**

Hermann Hesse was born in July 1877 in the little Swabian town of Calw, the son of Protestant missionaries. His home background and education were pietistic, intellectual, classical. He entered a theological seminary at the age of fourteen with the intention of taking orders and left two years later. In Basel he learned the book trade and made his living as a bookseller and editor of classical German literary texts. He became acquainted with Jacob Burckhardt, the great Swiss historian and philosopher, who later served as the model for the portrait of Father Jacobus in *The Bead Game*. In 1914 Hesse's "unpatriotic" antiwar attitude brought him official censure and newspaper attacks. Two months after the outbreak of the war, an essay entitled "O Freunde, nicht diese Töne" ("O Friends, not these tones") was published in the *Neue Zürcher Zeitung;* it was an appeal to the youth of Germany, deploring the stampede to disaster.

In 1911 he traveled in India. From 1914 to 1919 he lived in Bern, working in the German embassy as an assistant for prisoners of war. A series of personal crises accompanied the external crisis of the war: his father died; his youngest son fell seriously ill; his wife suffered a nervous breakdown and was hospitalized. In 1919, the year of the publication of *Demian,* he moved to the small village of Montagnola by the Lake of Lugano and remained there till the end of his life. In 1923 he

---

* Reprinted from *Psychedelic Review*, No. 3. This paper was coauthored by Ralph Metzner, editor of the *Review.*

acquired Swiss citizenship and in 1927 remarried. Hesse steeped himself in Indian and Chinese literature and philosophy, the latter particularly through the masterful translations of Chinese texts by Richard Wilhelm. In 1931 he remarried a third time and moved to another house in Montagnola which had been provided for him by his friend H. C. Bodmer. In 1946 he was awarded the Nobel Prize; in 1962, at the age of eighty-five, he died. Asked once what were the most important influences in his life, he said they were "the Christian and completely non-nationalist spirit of my parents' home," the "reading of the great Chinese masters," and the figure of the historian Jacob Burckhardt.

Few writers have chronicled with such dispassionate lucidity and fearless honesty the progress of the soul through the states of life. *Peter Camenzind* (1904), *Demian* (1919), *Siddhartha* (1922), *Steppenwolf* (1927), *Narziss und Goldmund* (1930), *Journey to the East* (1932), *Magister Ludi* (1943) —different versions of spiritual autobiography, different maps of the interior path. Each new step revises the picture of all the previous steps; each experience opens up new worlds of discovery in a constant effort to communicate the vision.

As John Cage is fond of reminding us, writing is one thing and reading is another. All writings, all authors are thoroughly misunderstood. Most wise men do not write because they know this. The wise man has penetrated through the verbal curtain, seen and known and felt the life process. We owe him our gratitude when he remains with us and tries to induce us to share the joy.

The great writer is the wise man who feels compelled to translate the message into words. The message is, of course, around us and in us at all moments. Everything is a clue. Everything contains all the message. To pass it on in symbols is unnecessary but perhaps the greatest performance of man.

Wise men write (with deliberation) in the esoteric. It's the way of making a rose or a baby. The exoteric form is maya, the hallucinatory facade. The meaning is within. The greatness of a great book lies in the esoteric, the seed meaning concealed behind the net of symbols. All great writers write the same book, changing only the exoteric trappings of their time and tribe.

Hermann Hesse is one of the great writers of our time. He wrote Finnegan's Wake *in several German versions. In addition to being a wise man, he could manipulate words well enough to win the Nobel Prize.*

Most readers miss the message of Hesse. Entranced by the pretty dance of plot and theme, they overlook the seed message. Hesse is a trickster. Like nature in April, he dresses up his code in fancy plumage. The literary reader picks the fruit, eats quickly, and tosses the core to the ground. But the seed, the electrical message, the code, is in the core.

Take *Siddhartha*[1]—the primer for young bodhisattvas, written when Hesse was forty-five. Watch the old magician warming up to his work. We are introduced to a proud young man, strong, handsome, supple-limbed, graceful. Siddhartha is young and ambitious. He seeks to attain the greatest prize of all—enlightenment. Cosmic one-upmanship. He masters each of the otherworldly games. The Vedas. Asceticism. Matches his wits against the Buddha himself. Tantric worldly success. "We find consolations, we learn tricks with which we deceive ourselves, but the essential thing—the way—we do not find." "Wisdom is not communicable." "I can love a stone, Govinda, and a tree or a piece of bark. These are things and one can love things. But one cannot love words. . . . Nirvana is not a thing; there is only the word Nirvana." Then in the last pages of the book, Hermann Hesse, Nobel Prize novelist, uses words to describe the wonderful illumination of Govinda, who

no longer saw the face of his friend Siddhartha. Instead he saw other faces, many faces, a long series, a continuous stream of faces—hundreds, thousands, which all came and disappeared and yet all seemed to be there at the same time, which all con-

tinually changed and renewed themselves and which were yet
all Siddhartha. He saw the face of a fish, of a carp, with
tremendous painfully opened mouth, a dying fish with dimmed
eyes. He saw the face of a newly born child, red and full of
wrinkles, ready to cry. He saw the face of a murderer, saw him
plunge a knife into the body of a man; at the same moment he
saw this criminal kneeling down, bound, and his head cut off
by an executioner. He saw the naked bodies of men and women
in the postures and transports of passionate love. He saw
corpses stretched out, still, cold, empty. He saw the heads of
animals, boars, crocodiles, elephants, oxen, birds. He saw
Krishna and Agni. He saw all these forms and faces in a
thousand relationships to each other, all helping each other,
loving, hating and destroying each other and become newly
born. Each one was mortal, a passionate, painful example of all
that is transitory. Yet none of them died, they only changed,
were always reborn, continually had a new face: only time
stood between one face and another. And all these forms and
faces rested, flowed, reproduced, swam past and merged into
each other, and over them all there was continually something
thin, unreal and yet existing, stretched across like thin glass or
ice, like a transparent skin, shell, form or mask of water—and
this mask was Siddhartha's smiling face which Govinda touched
with his lips at that moment. And Govinda saw that this mask-
like smile, this smile of unity over the flowing forms, this smile
of simultaneousness over the thousands of births and deaths—
this smile of Siddhartha—was exactly the same as the calm,
delicate, impenetrable, perhaps gracious, perhaps mocking,
wise, thousand-fold smile of Gotama, the Buddha, as he had
perceived it with awe a hundred times. It was in such a
manner, Govinda knew, that the Perfect One smiled.

*Those who have taken one of the psychedelic drugs may
recognize Govinda's vision as a classic LSD sequence. The direct
visual confrontation with the unity of all men, the unity of life.
That Hesse can write words such as* unity, love, Nirvana *is easily
understood. Every Hindu textbook gives you the jargon. But
his description of the visual details of the cosmic vision, the
retinal specifics, is more impressive. Whence came to Hesse*

these concrete sensations? The similarity to the consciousness-expanding drug experience is startling. The specific, concrete "is-ness" of the illuminated moment usually escapes the abstract philosopher of mysticism. Did Hesse reach this visionary state himself? By meditation? Spontaneously? Did H.H., the novelist himself, use the chemical path to enlightenment?

The answer to these questions is suggested in the next lesson of the master: *Steppenwolf*[2]—a novel of crisis, pain, conflict, torture—at least on the surface. Hesse writes in a letter: "If my life were not a dangerous painful experiment, if I did not constantly skirt the abyss and feel the void under my feet, my life would have no meaning and I would not have been able to write anything." Most readers sophisticated in psychodynamics recognize the drama presented—the conflict between ego and id, between spirit and material civilization, the "wolfish, satanic instincts that lurk within even our civilized selves," as the jacket of the paperback edition has it. "These readers [writes Hesse] have completely overlooked that above the Steppenwolf and his problematical life there exists a second, higher, timeless world . . . which contrasts the suffering of the Steppenwolf with a transpersonal and transtemporal world of faith, that the book certainly tells of pain and suffering but is the story of a believer not a tale of despair."

As in *Siddhartha*, Hesse involves the reader in his fantastic tale, his ideas, his mental acrobatics, only to show at the end that the whole structure is illusory mind play. The mental rug is suddenly pulled out from under the gullible psychodynamic reader. This Zen trick is evident on at least two levels in the *Steppenwolf*. First, in the little "Treatise," a brilliant portrait of Harry, the man with two souls: the man—refined, clever and interesting; and the wolf—savage, untamable, dangerous and strong. The treatise describes his swings of mood, his bursts of creativity, his ambivalent relationship to the bourgeoisie, his fascination with suicide, his inability to reconcile the two conflicting selves. A breathtakingly subtle psychological analysis. Then, the sleight of hand:

> There is . . . a fundamental delusion to make clear. All interpretation, all psychology, all attempts to make things comprehensible, require the medium of theories, mythologies and lies; and a self-respecting author should . . . dissipate these lies so far as may be in his power. . . . Harry consists of a hundred or a thousand selves, not of two. His life oscillates, as everyone's does, not merely between two poles, such as the body and the spirit, the saint and the sinner, but between thousands. . . . .
> Man is an onion made up of a hundred integuments, a texture made up of many threads. The ancient Asiatics knew this well enough, and in the Buddhist Yoga an exact technique was devised for unmasking the illusion of the personality. The human merry-go-round sees many changes: the illusion that cost India the efforts of thousands of years to unmask is the same illusion that the West has labored just as hard to maintain and strengthen.

The dualistic self-image is described—the fascinating and compelling Freudian metaphor—and is then exposed as a delusion, a limited, pitiful perspective, a mind game. The second example of this trick occurs at the end of the book. We have followed Hesse in his descriptions of Harry as he runs through a series of vain attempts to conquer his despair—through alcohol, through sex, through music, through friendship with the exotic musician Pablo; finally he enters the Magic Theater. "Price of Admission, your Mind." In other words, a mind-loss experience.

> From a recess in the wall [Pablo] took three glasses and a quaint little bottle. . . . He filled the three glasses from the bottle and taking three long thin yellow cigarettes from the box and a box of matches from the pocket of his silk jacket he gave us a light. . . . Its effect was immeasurably enlivening and delightful—as though one were filled with gas and had no longer any gravity.

Pablo says:

> You were striving, were you not, for escape? You have a long-
> ing to forsake this world and its reality and to penetrate to a
> reality more native to you, to a world beyond time. . . . You
> know, of course, where this other world lies hidden. It is the
> world of your own soul that you seek. Only within yourself
> exists that other reality for which you long. . . . All I can
> give you is the opportunity, the impulse, the key. I help you
> to make your own world visible. . . . This . . . theatre has
> as many doors into as many boxes as you please, ten or a hun-
> dred or a thousand, and behind each door exactly what you
> seek awaits you. . . . You have no doubt guessed long since
> that the conquest of time and the escape from reality, or how-
> ever else it may be that you choose to describe your longing,
> means simply the wish to be relieved of your so-called per-
> sonality. That is the prison where you lie. And if you enter the
> theatre as you are, you would see everything through the eyes
> of Harry and the old spectacles of the Steppenwolf. You are
> therefore requested to lay these spectacles aside and to be so
> kind as to leave your highly esteemed personality here in the
> cloak-room, where you will find it again when you wish. The
> pleasant dance from which you have just come, the treatise on
> the Steppenwolf, and the little stimulant that we have only this
> moment partaken of may have sufficiently prepared you.

It seems clear that Hesse is describing a psychedelic experience,
a drug-induced loss of self, a journey to the inner world. Each
door in the Magic Theater has a sign on it, indicating the endless possibilities of the experience. A sign called "Jolly Hunting.
Great Automobile Hunt" initiates a fantastic orgy of mechanical destruction in which Harry becomes a lustful murderer. A
second sign reads: "Guidance in the Building Up of the Personality. Success Guaranteed," which indicates a kind of chess game
in which the pieces are the part of the personality. Cosmic
psychotherapy. "We demonstrate to anyone whose soul has
fallen to pieces that he can rearrange these pieces of a previous
self in what order he pleases, and so attain to an endless multi-

plicity of moves in the game of life." Another sign reads: "All Girls Are Yours," and carries Harry into inexhaustible sexual fantasies. The crisis of the Steppenwolf, his inner conflicts, his despair, his morbidity and unsatisfied longing are dissolved in a whirling kaleidoscope of hallucinations. "I knew that all the hundred thousand pieces of life's game were in my pocket. A glimpse of its meaning had stirred my reason and I was determined to begin the game afresh. I would sample its tortures once more and shudder again at its senselessness. I would traverse not once more, but often, the hell of my inner being. One day I would be a better hand at the game. One day I would learn how to laugh. Pablo was waiting for me, and Mozart too."

So Harry Haller, the Steppenwolf, had his psychedelic session, discovered instead of one reality, infinite realities within the brain. He is admitted into the select group of those who have passed through the verbal curtain into other modes of consciousness. He has joined the elite brotherhood of the illuminati.

And then what? Where do you go from there? How can the holy sense of unity and revelation be maintained? Does one sink back into the somnambulent world of rote passion, automated action, egocentricity? The poignant cry of ex-league member H.H.: "That almost all of us—and also I, even I—should again lose myself in the soundless deserts of mapped out reality, just like officials and shop assistants who, after a party or a Sunday outing, adapt themselves again to everyday business life!" These are issues faced by everyone who has passed into a deep, transego experience. How can we preserve the freshness, illuminate each second of subsequent life? How can we maintain the ecstatic oneness with others?

Throughout the ages mystical groups have formed to provide social structure and support for transcendence. The magic circle. Often secret, always persecuted by the sleepwalking majority, these cults move quietly in the background shadows of history. The problem is, of course, the amount of structure surrounding the mystical spark. Too much too soon, and you have priesthood ritual on your hands. And the flame is gone. Too little, and the teaching function is lost; the interpersonal unity drifts into gaseous anarchy. The bohemians. The beats. The lonely arrogants.

Free from attachment to self, to social games, to anthropomorphic humanism, even to life itself, the illuminated soul can sustain the heightened charge of energy released by transcendent experiences. But such men are rare in any century. The rest of us seem to need support on the way. Men who attempt to pursue the psychedelic-drug path on their own are underestimating the power and the scope of the nervous system. A variety of LSD casualties results: breakdown, confusion, grandiosity, prima-donna individualism, disorganized eccentricity, sincere knavery and retreat to conformity. It makes no more sense to blame the drug for such casualties than it does to blame the nuclear process for the bomb. Would it not be more accurate to lament our primitive tribal pressures toward personal power, success, individualism?

Huston Smith has remarked that of the eightfold path of the Buddha, the ninth and greatest is right association. The transpersonal group. The consciousness-expansion community. Surround yourself after the vision, after the psychedelic session, with friends who share the goal, who can up-level you by example or unitive love, who can help reinstate the illumination.

The sociology of transcendence. Hesse takes up the problem of the transpersonal community in the form of the League of Eastern Wayfarers.[3]

"It was my destiny to join in a great experience. Having had the good fortune to belong to the League, I was permitted to be a participant in a unique journey." The narrator, H.H., tells that the starting place of the journey was Germany, and the time shortly after World War I. "Our people at that time were lured by many phantoms, but there were also many real spiritual advances. There were bacchanalian dance societies and Anabaptist groups, there was one thing after another that seemed to point to what was wonderful and beyond the veil." There were also scientific and artistic groups engaged in the exploration of consciousness-expanding drugs. Kurt Beringer's monograph *Der Meskalinrausch*[4] describes some of the scientific experiments and the creative applications. René Daumal's novel *Le Mont Analogue*[5] is a symbolic account of a similar league journey in France. The participants were experimenting widely with drugs such as hashish, mescaline and carbon tetrachloride.

Hesse never explicitly names any drugs in his writings, but the passages quoted earlier from the *Steppenwolf* are fairly unequivocal in stating that some chemical was involved and that it had a rather direct relationship to the subsequent experience. Now, after this first enlightenment, in *Journey to the East,* H.H. tells of subsequent visits to the Magical Theater.

> We not only wandered through Space, but also through Time. We moved towards the East, but we also traveled into the Middle Ages and the Golden Age; we roamed through Italy or Switzerland, but at times we also spent the night in the 10th century and dwelt with the patriarchs or the fairies. During the times I remained alone, I often found again places and people of my own past. I wandered with my former betrothed along the edges of the forest of the Upper Rhine, caroused with friends of my youth in Tübingen, in Basle or in Florence, or I was a boy and went with my school-friends to catch butterflies or to watch an otter, or my company consisted of the beloved characters of my books; . . . For our goal was not only the East, or rather the East was not only a country and something geographical, but it was the home and youth of the soul, it was everywhere and nowhere, it was the union of all times.

Later the link between the Steppenwolf's drug liberation and the league becomes more specific:

> When something precious and irretrievable is lost, we have the feeling of having awakened from a dream. In my case this feeling is strangely correct, for my happiness did indeed arise from the same secret as the happiness in dreams; it arose from the freedom to experience everything imaginable simultaneously, to exchange outward and inward easily, to move Time and Space about like scenes in a theatre.

Hesse is always the esoteric hand, but there seems to be little doubt that beneath the surface of his Eastern allegory runs the history of a real-life psychedelic brotherhood. The visionary experiences described in *Journey to the East* are identified by location and name of participants. A recently published biography[6] traces the connections between these names and locations and Hesse's friends and activities at the time.

> And again and again, in Swabia, at Bodensee, in Switzerland, everywhere, we met people who understood us, or were in some way thankful that we and our League and our Journey to the East existed. Amid the tramways and banks of Zürich we came across Noah's Ark guarded by several old dogs which all had the same name, and which were bravely guided across the dangerous depths of a calm period by Hans C., Noah's descendant, friend of the arts.

Hans C. Bodmer is Hesse's friend, to whom the book is dedicated, and who later bought the house in Montagnola for Hesse. He lived at the time in a house in Zurich named the Ark.

> One of the most beautiful experiences was the League's celebration in Bremgarten; the magic circle surrounded us closely there. Received by Max and Tilli, the lords of the castle. . . .

Castle Bremgarten, near Bern, was the house of Max Wassmer, where Hesse was often a guest. The "Black King" in Winterthur refers to another friend, Georg Reinhart, to whose house, "filled with secrets," Hesse was often invited. The names of

artists and writers which occur in *Journey to the East* are all
either directly the names of actual historical persons or immediately derived from them: Lauscher, Klingsor, Paul Klee, Ninon
(Hesse's wife), Hugo Wolf, Brentano, Lindhorst, etc. In other
words, it appears likely that the scenes described are based on
the actual experiences of a very close group of friends who met
in each other's homes in southern Germany and Switzerland
and pursued the journey to what was "not only a country and
something geographical, but it was the home and youth of the
soul, it was everywhere and nowhere, it was the union of all
times."

*So the clues suggest that for a moment in "historical reality"
a writer named Hermann Hesse and his friends wandered
together through the limitless pageants of expanded consciousness, down through the evolutionary archives. Then apparently
H.H. loses contact, slips back to his mind and his egocentric
perspectives. "The pilgrimage had shattered . . . the magic
had then vanished more and more." He has stumbled out of the
the life stream into robot rationality. H.H. wants to become an
author, spin in words the story of his life. "I, in my simplicity,
wanted to write the story of the league, I, who could not
decipher or understand one-thousandth part of those millions of
scripts, books, pictures and references in the archives!" Archives? The cortical library?*

*What then was, is, the league? Is it the exoteric society with a
golden-clad president, Leo, maker of ointments and herbal
cures, and a speaker, and a high throne, and an extended
council hall? These are but the exoteric trappings. Is not the
league rather the "procession of believers and disciples . . . in-
cessantly . . . moving towards the East, towards the Home of
Light"? The eternal stream of life ever unfolding. The unity of
the evolutionary process, too easily fragmented and frozen by
illusions of individuality. "A very slow, smooth but continuous
flowing or melting; . . . It seemed that, in time, all the substance from one image would flow into the other and only one
would remain . . ."*

Many who have made direct contact with the life process through a psychedelic or spontaneous mystical experience find themselves yearning for a social structure. Some external form to do justice to transcendental experiences. Hermann Hesse again provides us with the esoteric instructions. Look within. The league is within. So is the 2-billion-year-old historical archive, your brain. Play it out with those who will dance with you, but remember, the external differentiating forms are illusory. The union is internal. The league is in and around you at all times.

But to be human is to be rational. *Homo sapiens* wants to know. Here is the ancient tension. To be. To know. Well, the magician has a spell to weave here, too. The intellect divorced from old-fashioned neurosis, freed from egocentricity, from semantic reification. The mind illuminated by meditation ready to play with the lawful rhythm of concepts. The bead game.

The Bead Game (Magister Ludi),[7] begun in 1931, finished eleven years later, was published six months after its completion, but in Switzerland, not Germany. "In opposition to the present world I had to show the realm of mind and of spirit, show it as real and unconquerable; thus my work became a Utopia, the image was projected into the future, and to my surprise the world of Castalia emerged almost by itself. Without my knowledge, it was already preformed in my soul." Thus wrote Hesse in 1955. *The Bead Game* is the synthesis and end point of Hesse's developing thought; all the strands begun in *Siddhartha, Journey to the East, Steppenwolf* are woven together into a vision of a future society of mystic game players. The "players with pearls of glass" are an elite of intellectual mystics who, analogously to the monastic orders of the Middle Ages, have created a mountain retreat to preserve cultural and spiritual values. The core of their practice is the bead game, "a device that comprises the complete contents and values of our culture." The game consists in the manipulation of a complex archive of symbols and formulas, based in their structure on music and mathematics, by means of which all knowledge, science, art and culture can be represented.

> This Game of games . . . has developed into a kind of universal speech, through the medium of which the players are enabled to express values in lucid symbols and to place them in relation to each other. . . . A Game can originate, for example, from a given astronomical configuration, a theme from a Bach fugue, a phrase of Leibnitz or from the Upanishads, and the fundamental idea awakened can, according to the intention and talent of the player, either proceed further and be built up or enriched through assonances to relative concepts. While a moderate beginner can, through these symbols, formulate parallels between a piece of classical music and the formula of a natural law, the adept and Master of the Game can lead the opening theme into the freedom of boundless combinations.

The old dream of a *universitas,* a synthesis of human knowledge, combining analysis and intuition, science and art, the play of the free intellect, governed by aesthetic and structural analogies, not by the demands of application and technology. Again, on the intellectual plane, the problem is always just how much structure the mind game should have. If there are no overall goals or rules, we have ever-increasing specialization and dispersion, breakdown in communication, a Babel of cultures, multiple constrictions of the range in favor of deepening the specialized field. Psychology. If there is too much structure or overinvestment in the game goals, we have dogmatism, stifling conformity, ever-increasing triviality of concerns, adulation of sheer techniques, virtuosity at the expense of understanding. Psychoanalysis.

In the history of the bead game, the author explains, the practice of meditation was introduced by the League of Eastern Wayfarers in reaction against mere intellectual virtuosity. After each move in the game a period of silent meditation was observed; the origins and meanings of the symbols involved were slowly absorbed by the players. Joseph Knecht, the Game

Master, whose life is described in the book, sums up the effect as follows:

> The Game, as I interpret it, encompasses the player at the conclusion of his meditation in the same way as the surface of a sphere encloses its centre, and leaves him with the feeling of having resolved the fortuitous and chaotic world into one that is symmetrical and harmonious.

Groups which attempt to apply psychedelic experiences to social living will find in the story of Castalia all the features and problems which such attempts inevitably encounter: the need for a new language or set of symbols to do justice to the incredible complexity and power of the human cerebral machinery; the central importance of maintaining direct contact with the regenerative forces of the life process through meditation or other methods of altering consciousness; the crucial and essentially insoluble problem of the relation of the mystic community to the world at large. Can the order remain an educative, spiritual force in the society, or must it degenerate through isolation and inattention to a detached, alienated group of idealists? Every major and minor social renaissance has had to face this problem. Hesse's answer is clear: the last part of the book consists of three tales, allegedly written by Knecht, describing his life in different incarnations. In each one the hero devotes himself wholeheartedly to the service and pursuit of an idealist, spiritual goal, only to recognize at the end that he has become the slave of his own delusions. In "The Indian Life" this is clearest: Dasa, the young Brahmin, meets a yogi who asks him to fetch water; by the stream Dasa falls asleep. Later he marries, becomes a prince, has children, wages war, pursues learning, is defeated, hurt, humiliated, imprisoned, dies—and wakes up by the stream in the forest to discover that everything had been an illusion.

> Everything had been displaced in time and everything had been telescoped within the twinkling of an eye: everything was a dream, even that which had seemed dire truth and perhaps

also all that which had happened previously—the story of the prince's son Dasa, his cowherd's life, his marriage, his revenge upon Nala and his sojourn with the Yogi. They were all pictures such as one may admire on a carved palace wall, where flowers, stars, birds, apes and gods can be seen portrayed in bas-relief. Was not all that which he had most recently experienced and now had before his eyes—this awakening out of his dream of princehood, war and prison, this standing by the spring, this water bowl which he had just shaken, along with the thoughts he was now thinking—ultimately woven of the same stuff? Was it not dream, illusion, Maya? And what he was about to live in the future, see with his eyes and feel with his hands until death should come—was that of other stuff, of some other fashion? It was a game and a delusion, foam and dream, it was Maya, the whole beautiful, dreadful, enchanting and desperate kaleidoscope of life with its burning joys and sorrows.

The life of Joseph Knecht is described as a series of awakenings from the time he is "called" to enter the Castalian hierarchy ("Knecht" in German means "servant"), through his period as Magister Ludi, to his eventual renunciation of the order and the game. Castalia is essentially the league, frozen into a social institution. Again the trickster involves us in his magnificent utopian vision, the "Game of games," only to show at the end the transience of this form as of all others. Having reached the highest position possible in the order, Knecht resigns his post. He warns the order of its lack of contact with the outside world and points out that Castalia, like any other social form, is limited in time. In his justificatory speech he refers to "a kind of spiritual experience which I have undergone from time to time and which I call 'awakening.' "

I have never thought of these awakenings as manifestations of a God or a demon or even of an absolute truth. What gives them weight and credibility is not their contact with truth, their high origin, their divinity or anything in that nature, but their reality. They are monstrously real in their presence and inescapability, like some violent bodily pain or surprising natural phenomenon. . . . My life, as I saw it, was to be a transcendence, a progress from step to step, a series of realms to be traversed and left behind one after another, just as a piece of music perfects, completes and leaves behind theme after theme, tempo after tempo, never tired, never sleeping, always aware and always perfect in the present. I had noticed that, coincidental with the experience of awakening, there actually were such steps and realms, and that each time a life stage was coming to an end it was fraught with decay and a desire for death before leading to a new realm, and awakening and to a new beginning.

The mystic or visionary is always in opposition to or outside of social institutions, and even if the institution is the most perfect imaginable, the game of games, even if it is the one created by oneself, this too is transient, limited, another realm to be traversed. After leaving Castalia, Knecht wanders off on foot:

It was all perfectly new again, mysterious and of great promise; everything that had once been could be revived, and much that was new besides. It seemed ages since the day and the world had looked so beautiful, innocent and undismayed. The joy of freedom and independence flowed through his veins like a strong potion, and he recalled how long it was since he had felt this precious sensation, this lovely and enchanting illusion!

So there it is. The saga of H.H. The critics tell us that Hesse is the master novelist. Well, maybe. But the novel is a social form, and the social in Hesse is exoteric. At another level Hesse is the master guide to the psychedelic experience and its application. Before your LSD session, read *Siddhartha* and *Steppenwolf*. The last part of the *Steppenwolf* is a priceless manual.

Then when you face the problem of integrating your visions with the plastic-doll routine of your life, study *Journey to the East*. Find yourself a magic circle. League members await you on all sides. With more psychedelic experience, you will grapple with the problem of language and communication, and your thoughts and your actions will be multiplied in creative complexity as you learn how to play with the interdisciplinary symbols, the multilevel metaphors. *The bead game.*

But always, Hesse reminds us, stay close to the internal core. The mystic formulas, the league, the staggeringly rich intellectual potentials are deadening traps if the internal flame is not kept burning. The flame is of course always there, within and without, surrounding us, keeping us alive. Our only task is to keep tuned in.

Did Hesse Use Mind-Changing Drugs?

Although the argument of the preceding commentary does not depend on the answer to this question, there are sufficient clues in Hesse's writings to make the matter of some historical and literary interest. In Germany, at the time Hesse was writing, considerable research on mescaline was going on. This has been reported in a monograph by Kurt Beringer, *Der Meskalinrausch*. Much of the material was also analyzed in Heinrich Klüver's monograph, *Mescal*, the first book on mescaline published in English.*

In response to our inquiry, Professor Klüver, now at the University of Chicago, has written:

> To my knowledge Hermann Hesse never took mescaline (I once raised this question in Switzerland). I do not know whether he even knew of the mescaline experiments going on under the direction of Beringer in Heidelberg. You know, of course, that Hesse (and his family) was intimately acquainted with the world and ideas of India. This no doubt has colored many scenes in his books.

REFERENCES

[1] Hermann Hesse, *Siddhartha*, trans. by Hilda Rosner (New York, New Directions, 1957), pp. 20, 144, 147, 151–53.

[2] ——, *Steppenwolf*, trans. by Basil Creighton (New York, Random House, 1963), pp. vi, 62, 63, 66–67, 197–99, 217, 246.

[3] ——, *The Journey to the East*, trans. by Hilda Rosner (New York, Noonday Press, 1957), pp. 3, 10, 27–28, 29, 31, 96, 118.

* *Mescal: The "Divine" Plant and Its Psychological Effects* (University of Chicago Press, 1964).

[4] Kurt Beringer, *Der Meskalinrausch, seine Geschichte und Erscheinungsweise* (Berlin, Springer, 1927).

[5] René Daumal, *Mount Analogue: An Authentic Narrative,* trans. and intro. by Roger Shattuck; postface by Véra Daumal (New York, Pantheon, 1960).

[6] Bernhard Zeller, *Hermann Hesse: Eine Chronik in Bildern* (Frankfurt, Suhrkamp, 1960).

[7] Hermann Hesse, *Magister Ludi* (*The Bead Game*), trans. by Mervyn Savill (New York, Ungar, 1957), pp. 10, 17, 39, 355–56, 359, 367, 500–01.

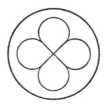

SEAL OF THE LEAGUE

11

*A Trip with Paul Krassner**

KRASSNER: I'd like to try not posing a single question you've ever been asked before.

LEARY: Okay, and I'll try not to give any answer I've ever given before.

KRASSNER: Do you think you would've been fired by Harvard for being AWOL if you hadn't conducted experiments with LSD that resulted in unfavorable publicity?

LEARY: Of course not.

KRASSNER: A lot of people smoke pot for what they consider pleasure, simply to get high. Are you copping out on them by fighting your marijuana case on the grounds of religious freedom?

LEARY: They have a perfect right to defend their use of marijuana or LSD as an instrument for getting high. The pursuit of happiness is the first sentence in the Declaration of Independence, which founded this republic. But most people who use LSD and marijuana to get high don't really know how to *do* it, because the science and discipline of ecstasy is probably *the* most demanding yoga that I can think of.

People who criticize my use of the First Amendment—that is, religious belief and practice—as a defense of my smoking marijuana and using LSD simply don't understand what religion *means,* or they have a very narrow Western, Protestant-Catholic-Jewish concept of religion.

---

* Reprinted from the *Realist,* September 1966.

My philosophy of life has been tremendously influenced by my study of oriental philosophy and religion. Of course, what the American, regardless of his religious belief, doesn't understand is that the aim of oriental religion is to *get high*, to have an ecstasy, to tune in, to turn on, to contact incredible diversity, beauty, living, pulsating meaning of the sense organs, and the much more complicated and pleasurable and revelatory messages of cellular energy.

To a Hindu, the spiritual quest is internal.

Different sects of oriental religion use different methods and different body organs to find God. The Shivites use the senses; the followers of Vishnu are concerned with cellular wisdom, contacting the endless flow of reincarnation wisdom which biochemists would call protein wisdom of the DNA code; Buddhist manuals on consciousness expansion are concerned with the *flash*, the white light of the void, the ecstatic union that comes when you're completely turned on, beyond the senses, beyond the body.

Another misconception about religion and my use of the First Amendment has to do with the institutional and establishment concept that Westerners have of religion. People that use marijuana and LSD in their own homes or their own gardens say, "What does this have to do with religion?" Because religion to them means priests, Bibles, churches, Sunday schools, sects, rules and regulations.

To most Orientals the sacred temple of religion is your own *body*. The shrine is in your own *home*. Your priest or teacher or guru is someone with whom you live and share most of the joys and frustrations of daily life.

There's another aspect of this religious definition of the cellular experience: it requires time, training, practice and discipline to really use your sense organs, to be able to focus in on your cells; to move your consciousness from one type of ecstasy to another requires knowledge and guidance.

To really use the instrument of your body and the millions of sensory and cellular cameras with which you're endowed requires know-how, and in the East these technical manuals are called textbooks of yoga or religious illumination.

So just turning on with pot or LSD in a spontaneous manner in your home can be pleasant and even revealing. For most people, it's a failure to pay respect to the potentialities of the nervous system and the cells and the powers of the psychedelic drugs like marijuana and LSD to open up these complex realms.

KRASSNER: Let's assume you win your case; what would be the implications for the pot smoker who wouldn't use religious freedom as a defense?

LEARY: It just so happened that I had been initiated by a Hindu guru, but you can join Art Kleps' Neo-American Church, you can declare your own religion with you and your wife. There is a lot of precedent, Supreme Court rulings, that religious beliefs and practices are an individual matter. The atheist who believes in pacifism can claim to be a conscientious objector. This was a monumental decision by Justice Douglas. I don't want to come on as a lawyer, but . . .

KRASSNER: Lenny Bruce did, why not you?

LEARY: Lenny did it, so why *should* I? But I would like to tell your readers that it's left to *them* to work out their solution, and if they believe in it, they will win.

The great lesson you learn from LSD, from contacting your cells, is that every generation has to reenact the whole evolutionary drama, and to live a full life you have to go through the *whole* sequence yourself. If you don't, you've sold out on the range of possibilities and challenges.

You have to be Moses, you have to hammer out your own ethical code. You have to be Bishop Berkeley and hammer out your solution to the problem of matter and idea. You have to be Plato. All the solutions you read about in textbooks are canned, static and meaningless.

You've got to fight your own defense of your religion because *every* man in history has to do it. Most people in history, most Americans, don't realize this and aren't *willing* to do it.

I'm fighting my case on the unique constellation of activities that I've engaged in—and it's a damn good case—but I would think that any pot smoker who *really understands* the potentialities of the energies he's releasing and the *power* of that benign plant he inhales has got a constitutional case.

If he doesn't understand it, he's just smoking pot, not for kicks, but because it's the hip game to play, and if that's the level he wants to stay on, then *he's* going to cop out, and he won't fight his case in his own mind or with the law.

KRASSNER: But don't you think that winning your case on religious grounds might preclude their legal right to smoke pot simply for kicks?

LEARY: My case is not based just on the religious belief. There are three issues involved:

My right to pursue my spiritual quests with the methods and the maps that make sense to me—that's the religious.

Number two, I have a right to pursue knowledge—not just because I'm a psychologist, but because a psychologist *should* be doing (most of them aren't) what *every* human being should be doing—trying to figure out, what is it all about? Pursuit of knowledge.

The third ground upon which I defend my use of marijuana is my right to live in my home and raise my kids and live my family life according to *my* best beliefs and my conscience.

So long as none of these three—religious, scientific or personal —activities produce any visible harm to my fellow man.

Now, the lawyers have picked up on the first—that is, the spiritual quest, or the religious issue—because as lawyers, they want to win the case, and there's a long tradition in our country of religious freedom. So there's *precedent* there.

I've had several debates with my lawyers. I've said, "Well, really, I'd rather go up on the *scientific* issue because most of my adult life has been devoted to this quest." They say, "Yes, but you're *really* writing totally new law there."

Granted that the Constitution should provide for the right to pursue knowledge, and it does—in religion. When you get to the right to raise your kids and to live your family life the way you want to, that may come into the Ninth Amendment, which is vaguely the constitutional right to privacy, but each of these issues requires an enormous amount of legal scholarship, and the lawyers have chosen the religious, admitting that the scientific and the personal will have *their* day in court.

I cannot fight all of these cases, and I cannot test all of the ambiguities and the blind spots in constitutional protection, but my case is going to be the first of *many* victories on all of these constitutional rights, which come down to the issue of if you want to smoke marijuana because you and your wife can make love more effectively that way, or because it tunes you on to music more, or because you enjoy your garden more, you have a constitutional right to *do* that. But I can't fight all these issues, and my lawyers can't.

We see this as a *broad* civil liberties campaign, and as I try to explain to my hipster friends, everything in life takes place cell by cell, step by step, and you have to win case by case. I predict that there will be *hundreds* of civil liberties cases concerning the right of an individual to change his own consciousness for *exactly* the goals and purposes that he wants.

See, I don't pretend to be a lawyer, but I do have a cellular, intuitive sense about where law, which is necessary to protect society, stops and where individual growth, which is necessary to keep society going, begins.

KRASSNER: Now your hipster friends will accuse you of copping out because you said that some day there'll come a case based on the right to smoke pot because a man and his wife can make love more effectively—you know, why do they have to be married?

LEARY: Well, the district attorneys were questioning children in my household today in a grand jury hearing about sleeping habits in my house, so we're already *into* that, but I'm sure that will come up.

KRASSNER: Someone in the Timothy Leary Defense Fund office earlier said, "Why, that's corrupting the morals of a minor. It's putting thoughts into her mind which might not have been there."

LEARY: They're there. Because the younger the person, the more in tune they are with their cells.

KRASSNER: I wonder if what I would call your form of mysticism isn't just a semantic difference between us. Now I believe that there are only individual consciousnesses; do you believe that God—or if you will, the universe—is conscious of its existence?

LEARY: I think that there are exquisite and complex harmonies at many different levels of energy in the universe and that this harmony involves a consciousness of the interwovenness of organic life and inorganic life. I think, though, that this incredible process of evolution is continually surprising itself and amazing itself and delighting itself and freaking itself out with what it's doing. But is there one central computer that's planning it all or can sum it all up in one moment? I don't think so.

KRASSNER: When you say "delighting itself, amazing itself," you're implying that there's an awareness of what it's doing.

LEARY: But it's out of control. There's an awareness not of what it's *doing;* there's an awareness of what's *happening.* God exists at every level of consciousness.

At the verbal symbolic level, God is the word g-o-d which is the center of the verbal network of the verbal mandala.

At the level of your senses, God is the central drone or the center of the sensory mandala—is the orgasm center, if you will.

At the level of cell, God is the DNA code because the DNA code, as biochemists describe it, is all the attributes that we have attributed to God: the all-powerful, ever-changing intelligence far greater than man's mind which is continually manifesting itself in different forms. Well, man, that's what the genetic code has been doing for 2 billion years.

Then very sophisticated biophysicists like Andrew Cochran tell us that so-called inorganic matter—molecules and atomic structures—have the same game going, that the nucleus of the atom is God at that level, it's always invisible, God is always the smallest and the most central. . . .

KRASSNER: Wait, before we get too abstract. What I'm really

asking boils down to this: You've gone on record as saying that you talk to trees; what I want to know is, do the trees hear what you're saying to them?

LEARY: Well, I hear what the trees are telling *me*. I *listen* to trees. Whether they hear me, I don't know. You'd have to ask a tree. I think they do.

There was an expert gardener in a little orchard we have at Millbrook, who was talking about cutting down some of the apple trees that I've been pruning and talking to for a couple of years now, because they're old and not producing and the apples are sour—he had all sorts of reasons. He wanted to bring in a lot of dwarf apples to make a lot of money.

I looked around and I said, "You realize this is a very reckless conversation you're involved in."

"Yeah, the trees can hear, right?"

And I said, "You notice that I've said nothing except friendly and protective things about these trees. There's no testimony from *me*. . . ."

Yes, I listen to the trees and hear what *they* say and I think that they hear what I say. Not what I *say*, since trees don't speak English, but the trees are very aware of what I'm doing to them and to the ground around them. And by me I don't mean Timothy Leary. They don't talk that language.

KRASSNER: Look, you're deaf in one ear, so if you lie with your good ear to the pillow, you can shut out sound—you can't hear a tree or a person. Now if a tree has no ears, by what process does it get your message?

LEARY: A tree doesn't speak in sound waves. When I listen to a tree, I don't listen with my ear. When I talk to the trees, I don't talk in words or language.

KRASSNER: But you really do believe that the tree is aware?

LEARY: Yes. When I walk out in any garden or field in Millbrook, I'm convinced that the vegetative life there is aware of my presence, and I'm sending out vibrations which they pick up.

KRASSNER: And somebody else would send out different vibrations?

LEARY: Yup.

KRASSNER: Then maybe there's truth to the old superstition that a menstruating woman can affect plant growth?

LEARY: I think it's possible. I would parenthetically suggest that we review a lot of so-called superstitions and primitive beliefs, and we'd find they're based upon cellular wisdom.

But you see, the embarrassing facts of the matter are that the DNA code which designed you is not that different from the DNA code that designed a tree. There are some obvious product-packaging differences, but they're both strands of living protein planfulness that go back to a common origin.

KRASSNER: But without the brain I would have no consciousness . . . or don't you accept that premise?

LEARY: My dear Paul, every cell in your *body* is acutely conscious, is decoding energy, has access to wisdom which dwarfs the mental, prefrontal symbolic aspect that you consider normal waking consciousness.

You called me a mystic, and you could call yourself a rationalist. I agree, you are a rationalist because you rely mainly on symbols. And you're a very acute and beautiful game analyst. But I don't consider myself a mystic; I consider myself a *real* realist in that I'm accepting the empirical evidence of modern biochemistry and the intuitive experiential evidence of what I've learned by taking LSD 300 times.

The Paul Krassner mind is about thirty years old, but there are energy systems, blueprinting facilities and memory systems within your cells and your nervous system which are hundreds of millions of years old, which have a language and a politics which are much more complicated than English and modern Democrat-Republican politics.

What we're doing for the mind is what the microbiologists did for the external sciences 300 years ago when they discovered the microscope. And they made this incredible discovery that life, health, growth, every form of organic life, is based on the cell, which is invisible.

You've never seen a cell; what do you think of that? Yet it's the key to everything that happens to a living creature. I'm simply saying that same thing from the mental, psychological standpoint, that there are wisdoms, lawful units inside the nervous system, invisible to the symbolic mind, which determine almost everything.

And I don't consider that mystical—unless you'd call someone who looks through a microscope a mystic, because he's telling you about something for which you don't have the symbols. Or the astronomer who detects a quasar and speculates about it.

KRASSNER: All right, but I don't consider it rationalistic to be hung up on symbols. I think we agree on the artificiality of symbols.

LEARY: Right.

KRASSNER: But I would go to the extent that a man perhaps could not be considered mentally healthy, or free—or cellular, to use your metaphor—if he couldn't . . . the most blatant example would be, let's say, if he couldn't spit on a crucifix just to show that the symbol itself is really an artifact.

LEARY: Yes, but in another sense I consider myself a rationalist because I believe that it is man's challenge to develop new symbol systems for these new levels of internal consciousness. Just as we had to develop a new symbol system for the invisible, uncharted world which was opened up with the microscope, the task now is to develop symbol systems for the new invisible worlds which are opened up by psychedelic drugs.

We're used to having many symbol systems on the macroscopic level. We use one symbol system for chess, another for baseball, another for politics. So is it necessary to have symbol systems for the different levels of consciousness.

Another fascinating challenge is to weave these multilevel symbol systems together into symphonic harmonies, which the psychiatrist would call hallucination and which I would call a fulfilled level of symphonic harmony, where you select the macroscopic symbol which fits the sensory orgasm, which harmonizes with the cellular dialect at the moment—you get them all flowing together.

And just as humor at the level of normal symbols is the juxtaposition of two game counters from different games, and we laugh, there's a cosmic humor in which you bring together inappropriate symbols from different levels. So with all the games we have going in the social-mental world, we can exquisitely complicate and multiply them in fascinating diversity as we add these new symbol systems, of the many senses and of the *infinite* number of cellular dialects.

KRASSNER: There's a slightly cosmic irony in all this. Because of the cutting off of LSD from reliable sources, the black market will increase, with inferior products as a result, so that some people may end up just getting a sort of escalated high, maybe higher than pot, but never experiencing the kind of profound insight into levels of reality that you talk about.

LEARY: I can't be terribly alarmed by that.

KRASSNER: Except that they might think, "We must be doing something wrong."

LEARY: Well, anyone who buys LSD on the black market and assumes that he's buying what the seller tells him he's getting, unless he *knows* that seller, is naïve.

Or the person who has an LSD session in a surrounding which is ugly and disharmonious, whether that be a psychiatric clinic or a pad or a penthouse, is naïve and foolish.

I can't take the responsibility for, or devote any of my energy to, lamenting the inevitable torrent of millions of unprepared, foolishly organized LSD sessions. More than anyone else in the world, I've been lecturing to the point of exhaustion to tell people to know what they're doing.

KRASSNER: On the other hand, is there a danger from an overdose?

LEARY: No. There's no such thing as an overdose of LSD. There's no known lethal quantity. Obviously, the more you take, the harder the first hit. But another one of the beautiful things about LSD, it even up-levels the numbers game on dosage, once you get beyond 100, 200 gamma. It's very hard to play games with LSD within the quantity game.

But if someone buys a sugar cube and finds that they're getting a pot high, they should realize that they've just gotten enough, maybe 25 or 50 gamma, which is going to bring them to the sensory level, and enjoy it, and not feel there's something wrong with *me* that I can't find God in the pill, what's going on? Common sense and careful preparation will guide you through these dilemmas.

In the early days of LSD research, we all had to struggle with these problems. In the early days of any new form of energy, you run into these problems. When you think of the reckless danger of unprepared people who went in those canvas and wood airplanes that the Wright brothers turned up, that was absolute madness, but they did it and they had a *right* to do it, knowing they were taking a risk.

In the early days of our research, I took all sorts of strange drugs that came from the South Seas and from South America and from Morocco to find out what they did and about dosage.

The early people who discovered the microscopes, before they really knew how to grind lenses, were getting different amplifications and flaws in the lens. There's no security and there's no guarantee of complete safety in life—and the realistic attitude, the scientific attitude, is to check out, recognize, compare, but keep *doing* it, because you're only going to learn by trial and error.

KRASSNER: Recently I spoke at Harvard Law School, and when someone asked about the five-year-old girl who accidentally ate an LSD sugar cube left in the refrigerator by her uncle, I replied that she's back in school now and was assigned to write a composition called "My Trip."

LEARY: Is that true?

KRASSNER: No, I was being facetious, but the significant thing is that you thought it might be possible.

LEARY: Well, first of all, about that little girl, the facts of the matter are that she is back in school, she was discharged from the hospital and there's no evidence that she was harmed. The scandal of that case was not the poor uncle, who left his cube around and was made to feel guilty and criminal about it; the scandal of that case were the politically minded doctors and district attorneys who made dramatic announcements about danger and "ruined for life."

We don't know what the effect would be on a little girl, and from all of the evidence so far, we would be led to believe that her reaction to that LSD depends entirely upon the attitude of the adults around her, and if when they discovered that she'd taken LSD, they treated it as a rare opportunity and turned off *their* fear and *their* guilt and *their* selfishness as bad mothers and bad uncles and bad fathers, and spent the next 12 hours really being *with* that kid, it would have been a glorious experience.

Even under the circumstances of ruthlessly dragging this poor little girl down to the hospital, pumping her stomach—which has *no* medical meaning because the LSD takes over within a few seconds and is metabolized very quickly (of course that's just to make the doctors feel better, pumping out the girl's stomach) —even in spite of all that, there were points where she was alternately laughing and crying. Well, I could understand that; I'd be doing the same.

But in spite of all of the brutal mishandling and the selfish copping out on almost everyone's part—I can't comment on the uncle or the parents because I don't know what they did—but the public health officials who were protecting their interests and using this as part of their campaign, *still* there's no reason to believe that this girl won't look back on it in the future as a great experience and that she won't be more likely to be a tuned-in, turned-on person in the future. There's more chance of that than there is that there'll be any damage, in spite of the emotional brutality to which she was subjected.

KRASSNER: Do you think that drugs will be given to young children some day?

LEARY: In general, I predict that psychedelic drugs will be used in all schools in the very near future as educational devices —not only drugs like marijuana and LSD, to teach kids how to use their sense organs and their cellular equipment effectively, but new and more powerful psychochemicals like RNA and other proteins which are really going to revolutionize our concepts of ourselves and education.

So that the notion about writing an essay in the first grade on your trip is not just science fiction, it's definitely going to happen. People should learn to use their nervous system and their cellular equipment before they're taught reading and writing and symbolic techniques. Because if you don't know how to handle your *native* equipment, you're going to be addicted to, and limited by, the artifacts of symbols.

I intend to have more children, and I'll tell you this, that I'm not going to push symbols on my kids—I won't keep anything *away* from them, but I'm not going to push symbols on my kids till they're ten, twelve, maybe fifteen years old.

I will never encourage them to read a book. I will encourage them to tune in on their own internal vocabularies and cellular Libraries of Congress. I'll teach them how to live as an animal and as a creature of nature and decode and communicate with the many energies around them, before I will force artifactual symbols—which are only 200 or 300 years old at best—on their 2-billion-year-old cellular machineries. And my kids feel the same way and will probably be doing that with *their* children.

KRASSNER: Can you see that being declared unconstitutional in a case brought by a psychedelic Madalyn Murray, claiming that it's a violation of separation of church and state, and that she doesn't mind if kids take LSD at home but it shouldn't be compulsory in public schools?

LEARY: Well, it's conceivable, and of course Madalyn Murray is playing a fascinating role in society today testing out game situations. I don't intend to send my future children to schools. I'd rather have them take heroin than go to a first-grade grammar school in this country.

KRASSNER: Would you set any age limit—working backward chronologically—as to a child taking LSD?

LEARY: I think this has to be tested. LSD should be used at that moment when the kid's symbol system freezes, because what LSD does is allow you to unhook and regroup your symbol system. I have no evidence on this, but I hope in the future that we will have.

KRASSNER: [Scene II: Millbrook, a week later] Here's a typical reporter's question: How do you feel about your indict-

ment in Poughkeepsie this morning for possession of marijuana?

LEARY: It had almost no effect on me. I would've been more
interested to learn that the Mets had won their third straight
game, probably because I know I'm probably never going to
come to trial and that I'm not terribly involved in the legal
technicalities.

KRASSNER: Being back here in Millbrook, I was thinking about
your second wife. I assume you took LSD together—reimprinting on each other every week—increasing the depth of your
relationship. And yet the marriage broke up on the honeymoon
trip. . . .

LEARY: As I said when I was on trial in Laredo and I was
asked who gave me the pot, I'll be glad to describe any of my
own experiences, but I don't want to make any comments
which involve other people. Any comments about my marriage
would be involving someone who's very dear and sacred to me,
whose privacy should not be violated.

KRASSNER: I appreciate that. The relevance I had in mind
was the apparent failure of LSD imprinting.

LEARY: I'll be glad to talk about the effects of imprinting on
interpersonal relationships. I consider this the most important
aspect of the LSD challenge—the business of imprinting and
reimprinting.

Every time you take LSD you completely suspend—you step
outside of—the symbolic chessboard which you have built up
over the long years of social conditioning. And you whirl
though different levels of neurological and cellular energy,
continually flowing and changing.

Your symbolic mind is flashing in and out. You never *lose*
your mind during an LSD session. It's always there, but it's one
of a thousand cameras that are flashing away. Of course, the
LSD freak-out, or paranoia, is where the symbolic mind freezes
any aspect of the LSD session and defines a new reality, which
can be positive or negative.

And toward the end of an LSD session you begin to re-
imprint. This is a very crucial time in the LSD session because

you take a new picture of yourself, of the world and of the people around you, both real and remembered. It's particularly tricky, because what you're doing during this imprinting period is getting a new perspective of yourself and the other people. Now this is tricky, because you may come out of an LSD session with a very different picture of yourself.

If the LSD session has been microscopically revealing of your own shortcomings and you're not experienced enough to be able to let this flow, too, and accept these aspects in yourself as a fragmentary part of a great, endlessly changing design, then you come out depressed. You've taken a bad picture of yourself. This accounts for the LSD depression, which can last for many days and for many months.

You can also take a negative picture of LSD itself, and you come out of the session saying, "Never again." So the challenge, number one, is to make a neurological contract with yourself that you're not going to take too finally and dogmatically any picture that you click or come out with during an LSD session because you have to dedicate yourself to the ongoing yoga of taking LSD many times, and not copping out just because you've taken one bad picture. If you do that, you have lost the opportunity to continue to use your neurological camera.

Now the same thing is true if you have an LSD session with somebody else, particularly with your wife or with a person with whom you have an ongoing relationship. It's perfectly possible after any LSD session to come out with a *negative* picture of the other person. You may have had many LSD sessions with someone, but that 13th session may close on a note of horror.

A natural reaction, of course, after this is to say, "Well, I never want to take LSD with that person again," because of that last freaky session. That is, from the standpoint of neurological ethics, a game violation. The neurological contract should have provisions for continuing the sessions together until you get to that point where you're both convinced that you've explored all the relevant areas in each other and in the relationship.

KRASSNER: There's a man who shall remain nameless who has

taken LSD and continues his game of professional war planning for the Pentagon. . . .

LEARY: Why don't you name him?

KRASSNER: I don't want to betray a confidence.

LEARY: Can I name him?

KRASSNER: If you want to, sure.

LEARY: Herman Kahn.

KRASSNER: Aren't you violating his privacy?

LEARY: That's no confidence. I didn't give him LSD. Many people I know have told me about his taking LSD.

KRASSNER: Each one of whom he told in confidence, probably.

LEARY: Do you think the time has come to share with a waiting world the names of the prominent people whose lives have been changed by taking LSD?

KRASSNER: If you don't think it's unethical, I think the time has come.

LEARY: That's why I admire Steve Allen. Because he has not let his narrower secular games—and they're highly sensitive, public and even political now—interfere with his basic integrity. He has said on television that he has taken LSD and it was the most important experience of his life. The main question is whether in the Senate hearings on May 25th [*due to legal problems Leary was unable to testify*] I should illustrate the effectiveness of LSD by describing the positive effects on famous people who have used LSD.

I testified in Washington last week before the Senate Juvenile Delinquency Committee. I brought down my son and daughter to sit next to me, for many reasons. I wanted them to share my—they've been in jail with me, they've been deported from several countries with me, they were indicted with me—they might as well live through the paranoia of the Senate hearings with me; but also as a living illustration of two famous juvenile delinquents—my daughter, eighteen, who is under a heavy sentence at the present time, and my son, sixteen, who has been arrested and jailed ten times.

During these hearings, a police captain [Alfred Trembly] from Los Angeles went through the same dreary dance of the cases that his agents had arrested during LSD sessions. He was reading from case histories—"We received a tip from an informer about an LSD party on a beach near Los Angeles. Two of my agents discovered two men sitting by the ocean staring out over the sea. As they approached and the two men saw them coming, they fell upon their knees, and when the agents walked up to them, they turned up and said, 'We love you.' At this point, or shortly thereafter, the two men ran into the water, and my police officers had to rush into the tide to save their lives."

Now I was sitting next to my two children at these hearings, and as each of these so-called horror stories developed, we leaned back and said, "Why, of course, we understand exactly how and why such highly harmonious and natural developments would occur, like falling on your knees at the approach of two police officers."

I realize that Senator Dodd and Senator Kennedy were much more impressed by these stories of horror, so that when I testified about the philosophic and political realities involved, my testimony seemed tame and professorial, and that's why I'm suggesting that perhaps at the next Senate hearing, I should bring some case histories of my own.

One would illustrate how Bill Wilson, who founded Alcoholics Anonymous, has told many of his friends that LSD is a natural and inevitable cure for alcoholism.

Or I could tell the interesting case history of Chuck Dederich, who founded Synanon—and this is not a breach of confidence, by the way. He's told reporters that the insights which cured his alcoholism and led to the founding of the only institutional cure for heroin addiction came from his LSD session.

Or I could tell the story of Herman Kahn, who by the way is often misunderstood, but Herman is not a war planner, he's a civil defense planner. Herman's claim is that he is one of the few highly placed Americans who's willing to gaze with naked eyes upon the possibilities of atomic warfare and come up with solutions to this horrible possibility. Perhaps his LSD sessions have given him this revelation and courage. And even his phrase "spasm war," which to the intellectual liberal sounds gruesome, is a powerful, cellular metaphor describing an event which the very phrase itself, "spasm war," might prevent.

Or I could remind the Senate and the American public of Cary Grant, whose first child was born in his sixties after renewal and revigorations which he attributes to LSD.

Or I could mention Henry Luce and Clare Boothe Luce, two Americans whose power and game-playing skill can hardly be discounted and who have always been obsessed with a religious quest, both of whom have taken LSD many times.

KRASSNER: Which may well be why *Life* magazine had a let's-not-be-too-hasty editorial. But you can't really generalize about this wound between the generations, then.

LEARY: I testified in Washington last week before the Senate Juvenile Delinquency Committee. I was welcomed by Senator Dodd with affectionate and respectful comments, and then I began my short statement, which had to do with the breakdown of communication between the generations, the middle-aged and the young. And just as I was toward the end of this, Teddy Kennedy—who had rushed back into town unexpectedly to appear at these televised hearings—interrupted me by saying, "Mr. Leary, I don't understand what you're talking about." Exactly!

KRASSNER: That's because he doesn't know which generation to identify with.

LEARY: That's the particular problem I was talking about, the breakdown of communication. But I was disturbed by the obvious hostility on the part of Edward Kennedy. He didn't know what he was talking about. He hadn't researched the subject because I can be challenged on many levels on many issues. This seemed to be an unprepared and instinctive attack on Teddy Kennedy's part, upon what he obviously felt was an unpopular and non-vote-getting position.

I was disturbed by this because I've been saying over and over again that the position that one takes on the LSD controversy and the sexual freedom issue is the most perfectly predicted by the person's age. A Supreme Court of seventeen-year-olds would never have convicted Ralph Ginzburg.

KRASSNER: I think you're wrong. It depends on which seventeen-year-olds. The ones you and I know wouldn't have, but I don't think you can be that rigid. . . .

LEARY: I'm obviously wrong, because Teddy Kennedy is one of the youngest members of the Senate, whom I would hopefully expect to be most alert to the needs and impulses of the younger generation. He proved to be hostile, whereas Senator Dodd, much his senior, was courteous, although bewildered.

KRASSNER: Dr. Nathan Kline was quoted in *Newsweek:* "Under drugs like pot you tend to feel that you love everyone and the world is a great place. And if anyone wants to go to bed with you, it's just one more great experience to share. Pregnancy becomes the most frequent side effect of pot." Now, you've said that the closer one communicates with his cells—with or without consciousness-expanding drugs—one knows when one is making a baby. How would you reconcile—

LEARY: Well, pot does not turn you on to your cells; pot turns you on to your senses. It's true that marijuana is a fantastically effective aphrodisiac, and the person who understands pot can weave together a symphony of visual, auditory, olfactory, gustatory, tactual sensitivity to make lovemaking an adventure which dwarfs the imagination of the pornographers.

This has nothing to do with pregnancy.

I would suggest that before believing what Dr. Kline says about marijuana, we ask him, has he ever smoked it, and has he done a serious study of the effects of this fascinating and holy drug? The answer, of course, would be no.

I would say that the drug that gets you knocked up, blindly and unconsciously, is alcohol. Alcohol does reduce inhibitions—people become aggressive, indiscriminately loving *or* hostile, weeply self-pitying or self-expansive. Alcohol stimulates the social emotions, and it's well-known that alcohol is a seductive instrument which will produce round heels in any woman.

This has nothing to do with sensual enhancement, which marijuana produces. Alcohol dulls the senses, reduces everything to a crude wrestling match. I would say that alcohol has produced more unplanned pregnancies than any drug around.

Under marijuana, with your senses *heightened,* you're not about to go to bed with a crude seducer.

KRASSNER: And yet, for some, pot has taken the place of alcohol as part of the seduction process.

LEARY: Yes, but it's a much higher-level form of seduction. It's not seduction at all, it's a highly intricate, delicate, exquisite enhancer of communication. If you have an alcoholic man coming on to a girl who is smoking marijuana, nothing's going to happen except the horrified shrinking back on the part of the marijuana smoker.

KRASSNER: According to the *Wall Street Journal,* "Hallucinatory drugs, including LSD, have joined nerve gases and a multitude of disabling germs in the nation's arsenal of chemical and biological weapons. . . ."

LEARY: The fascinating thing about LSD is that everyone wants to control it.

The person who doesn't want to use it wants to control it so nobody else can use it. The cops want to take it away from youngsters and put them in jail for controlling it and keep it themselves. The researchers want it to do research; the psychiatrists want it as an adjunct to psychotherapy. I've had dozens of ministers tell me, "This is an authentic religious experience, but its use in any other context except the spiritual is a sacrilege." The artist wants to control it to win the Nobel Prize.

No matter *why* they want to use it, what *gain* they have that's going to be facilitated by it, they all want to have it in their hands. And I, for one, think they're *all* right, that *everyone* should have it in their little hot hands, for whatever use they want.

And another statement about LSD came in the Senate committee hearing when Senator Dodd said, "Well, this material *has* to be controlled because I understand it's odorless, colorless, and . . ." He started fumbling, and I said, "Tasteless, Senator Dodd." He said, "Oh, yes, tasteless."

I said, "Senator Dodd, in addition to that, it's *free.* You can make 20,000 doses of LSD for about a hundred dollars, which means that LSD is less expensive than pure water itself"—and at this point I held up a glass of water. He said, "All the more reason to control it." I said, "Yes, Senator, and all the clearer that you can't *possibly* control it."

KRASSNER: Every time I laugh I get high.

LEARY: Laughing is definitely antiadministration.

KRASSNER: A couple of years ago you told me that the free-speech movement in Berkeley was playing right onto the game boards of the administration and the police, and that the students could shake up the establishment much more by just staying in their rooms and changing their nervous systems. But now that you're involved in the fighting-the-law game, do you still feel that way?

LEARY: Yes. Any external or social action, unless it's based on expanded consciousness, is a robot behavior—including political action in favor of LSD and marijuana.

And you will notice that I have not suggested traditional political action in defense of marijuana and LSD. I'm involved in legal action to protect myself and other people from going to jail. But my attitude toward this legal skirmishing is extremely detached.

My advice to myself and to everyone else, particularly young people, is to turn on, tune in and drop out. By drop out, I mean to detach yourself from involvement in secular, external social games. But the dropping out has to occur *internally* before it occurs externally. I'm not telling kids just to quit school; I'm not telling people just to quit their jobs. That is an inevitable development in the process of turning on and tuning in.

Mostly all social decisions are made on the basis of symbolic pressure—symbolic reactions. Most men and women who drop out of the secular game to become monks and nuns are doing it under the pressure of freaky sexual or social game harassments. Such decisions are blind and unconscious.

American society's an insane and destructive enterprise. But before you can take any posture in relationship to this society, you have to sanitize yourself internally. Then you drop out, not in rebellion but as an act of harmony.

My comments about the student rebellion, and even the civil

rights movement, stem from these convictions. I have no interest in students rebelling against university authorities to make a better university, because they can't. I have no sympathy with a civil rights movement which attempts to "raise" the Negro to the level of the middle-class white American.

The university is an institution for consciousness contraction, and any attempt to give students more power and responsibility in running universities is a growth of collective insanity. The most hopeful development in the last 10 years has been the dropout phenomenon. This is unique in human history.

For thousands of years the goal of children of poor people, of politically impoverished people, has been to get more education, because education means power, wealth, control. Now for the first time we have a generation which is dropping out—a tremendously exciting, revolutionary symptom.

It means to me that many of the young people are dealing themselves *out* of the power game and the control game.

Instead of picketing university administration buildings, I think young people should first turn on, then tune in, and then walk off the campus. While I have great sympathy for the draft-card burners, I would still prefer them to sit in front of a psychedelic shrine in their own home and burn a dollar bill. Or, as the ironic John Bircher has suggested, burn their Social Security cards.

KRASSNER: I want to relate "The Spring Grove Experiment" which we watched on TV to your comments about turning on and dropping out. Now one of the patients, an alcoholic, was given LSD in a psychotherapeutic context, and his cure—as far as the program was concerned—was dropping in.

LEARY: Right. He was going to night school, learning—of all things—accounting, and he was going to get a better job. [*Leary makes a strange sound.*]

KRASSNER: I won't know how to spell that.

LEARY: B-r-e-u-o-o-o-g-h! That's what I just said, which is Vishnu's laugh of cosmic horror.

Sanford Unger [*the psychiatrist on the CBS-TV show*] took LSD the first time in my house at Newton five years ago. Half-way through the session, he sat up in the room, and he said to me something to this effect: *"Whooooo-osh!* What do we do now? Where do we go with this? How do we get it across to people?"

Now there are several ways in which you can diagnose one of our graduates in the LSD profession. If they sit on the floor with a patient, they're one of our graduates. If they hold hands with or touch the patient physically during the session, they're one of our graduates. If they use religious and philosophic metaphors, they're one of our graduates, and you will note all of these themes running through the television program tonight. The psychiatric approach to the selling of the psychedelic experience is like selling Christ because He makes you happier, gets you a better job, makes you more money. Everyone receives the message of LSD at the level to which their receptive apparatus is tuned, and I've no objection to and considerable admiration for the mental health approach. Although it's shortsighted, narrow, it obviously gets to more people in the middle-aged bracket than *I* get to; I horrify and terrorize middle-aged people.

And you'll notice that the theme of that TV show was pitched directly to the heart of the middle-aged neurosis—the meaninglessness of life, the breakdown of communication with the husband, the feeling of emptiness and being a fake, the feeling of having consistently failed, the notion of "Can I die and be reborn again?" These are the spiritual and psychological terrors of the middle-aged, and Dr. Sanford Unger and his television collaborators accurately sensed and effectively talked *to* these anguishing dilemmas.

KRASSNER: What did you learn from your spiritual quest in India?

LEARY: I spent four months on my honeymoon in a little cottage on a ridge which looked out at the Himalayas. This cottage had no electricity, gas or water, and was rented from the Methodist Church, which also supplied a Moslem cook, who also supplied me once a week, after his shopping trip to the village, with a finger-size stick of attar or hashish.

This was one of the most serene and productive periods of my life. I spent at least two hours a day in meditation, an hour of which was facilitated by the use of this excellent village-grown and hand-rolled hashish. And I spent 1 day a week, as I have for the last 6 years, in an LSD session. I spent about 2 hours a day listening to Lama Anargarika Govinda talk about the *I Ching* and Tibetan yoga. And I spent several hours a day thinking about how man can get back into harmonious interaction with nature.

During this period I worked out very detailed notes and blueprints for the next 500 years. It's an interesting thing about man and man's mind and man's intellectual productions. Rarely if ever have men produced a blueprint for the future which goes beyond their own life.

We are encouraged at the present time in America to revere and admire such far-seeing organizations as Rand Corporation, which is planning our military defense as far as 10 years ahead. Occasionally, in the last hundred years, men called conservationists have pleaded with legislators to pay some attention to our rape of the rivers, forests, prairies, and skies. Until very recently, such men were considered kooks and far-out do-gooders.

Before I went to India, I talked to many men who are in strategic planning positions in our intellectual establishment—the top officials of Xerox and IBM, for example—and I asked them, who's planning for the future? Are the Chinese Communists? Are the Russians? Are we? Now it's possible, and I hope it's probable, that there are secret agencies in our government, and the Chinese government, planning for the future, but I doubt it. And furthermore, I suspect that whatever planning is done is at the lowest level of imperialistic politics.

It's my ambition to be the holiest, wisest, most beneficial man alive today. Now this may sound megalomaniac, but I don't see why. I don't see why every one of your readers, every person who lives in the world, shouldn't have that ambition. What else should you try to be? The president of the board, or the chairman of the department, or the owner of this and that?

KRASSNER: But why not drop out of even that?

LEARY: I'm ready. And do *what?* You've got to name me a

better game. And this has been my challenge for the last six years. I'm ready to give up LSD at a moment's notice if someone will suggest to me a game which is more exciting, more promising, more expansive, more ecstatic. Tell me, Paul. I'll take off my shoes and follow you.

KRASSNER: Suppose I suggest the possibility of a better game—which I might not have been qualified to do a year ago, because I hadn't taken LSD yet, but I've had it three times now, which gives me the arrogance to ask—wouldn't a better game, ideally, be to do it without LSD?

LEARY: Yes, that's part of my plan. LSD . . . what is LSD? LSD is not a thing, a drug. LSD is simply a key to opening up sensory, cellular and precellular consciousness so that you flow and harmonize with these different levels.

Now if we understood how to raise children so that they wouldn't be addicted to symbols and they wouldn't be addicted to stupefacient drugs such as television, alcohol, then we wouldn't need LSD. Nature always produces the cure for the particular disease which has evolved.

The disease that is crushing and oppressing this planet today is man's possessive and manipulatory symbolic mind and the cure for the disease has been provided. I have no illusions. I've *never* made any great claims for LSD. It's simply a particular evolutionary molecule at exactly that moment when it's needed.

The young generation needs LSD to cure the symbolic plague. Their children won't need LSD except for the mentally ill. The mentally ill in the second generation to come will be those who get addicted to symbols, power.

Some of my visionary colleagues think that we're going to have to kill the members of our species who get addicted to control and power in the future. I don't. I think that LSD treatment will bring them back in harmony.

But the third generation from now will not need LSD. The fourth generation from now will be in such perfect harmony with every form of molecular, cellular, seed and sensory energy that LSD will be unnecessary.

KRASSNER: Aren't you ignoring human nature?

LEARY: What do you mean by human nature?

KRASSNER: I mean—in addition to all the cooperative and compassionate qualities—the orneriness, the power drives, the aggressiveness, the hostility that realistically . . .

LEARY: Who are you to say what's real?

KRASSNER: I'm describing what exists by my perception.

LEARY: It is an unfortunate aspect of recent human history that those human beings who are addicted or driven to power, control and murder have tried to kill off the gentle, harmonious, open people. But they haven't; they've just pushed them underground. The present spasm of control, power and murder is *not* human nature.

It is true that as animals, and as carnivorous animals, we have had to kill to live. And it's true at every level of life that species have to eat each other, species have to combat each other to find their place in the overall scheme. But this is a harmonious and fully conscious procedure.

Now you called me on my eating steak in New York the other night. I feel that part of me *is* mammalian and does demand and need animal fiber. In my plan for the future, there will be some carnivorous activity. We will be food-conscious, and we'll pay respect to the rights of the other species.

As a matter of fact, starting next week, we're going to have animals on this property here in Millbrook. Some of these animals we will raise to slaughter, but we will not kill these animals until we know them well and have had LSD sessions with them, until we have seen that they have produced offspring. We will then preserve their offspring.

We will keep the sacred soul of the animal alive, because the soul of the living organism is its genetic code, and it's perfectly natural and right that one species eat another species as long as they don't wipe the species out.

Now man's use of animals, when you raise them just for slaughter—anonymously, impersonally and in robot fashion—produces a robot species, which is modern civilized man. In a fully conscious society, we're aware of the fact that we're going to have to eat each other.

My plan for Millbrook and my blueprint for the world is that we will exist in harmonious, interspecies interactions. I plan to have in Millbrook this spring members of 7 species, who'll all be feeding off each other and supporting each other. We'll have fungi, plants, insects, amphibia, reptiles, fish, mammals.

We'll feed each other, we'll protect each other, we'll protect each other's offspring and we'll build up a cycle of interspecies harmony and mutual collaboration. And we'll pay respect to the facts that the symbolic human mind can't face—one, that we all die; two, that we all eat each other; three, we must all provide for each other's genetic or soul growth.

So I see no ambiguities or conflicts in the plan which I suggest and what *you* say is human nature I see as a freaky, recently faddist and, in the long run, irrelevant tendency to blindly, ruthlessly destroy other forms of human life and other forms of species life on this planet, which in the long run is obviously suicidal.

Human nature is like every other nature of living creature on this planet, basically alert, open, conscious, collaborative.

KRASSNER: And competitive.

LEARY: And competitive, right. But there's a difference between competition and murder. The New York Yankees compete with the Washington Senators and they don't want to kill them with baseball bats, because they realize that if the Yankees were to beanball and baseball-bat out of existence the Senators, there'd be no more game of baseball.

And that, dear Paul, is the lesson of evolution which my cells have taught me. Balance: competition, mutual cannibalism and, above all, protection of the young of all species.